D1478305

The Invention of Shakespeare,
and Other Essays

The Invention of Shakespeare, and Other Essays

Stephen Orgel

PENN

UNIVERSITY OF PENNSYLVANIA PRESS

PHILADELPHIA

Published by
University of Pennsylvania Press
Philadelphia, Pennsylvania 19104-4112
www.upenn.edu/pennpress

Printed in the United States of America on acid-free paper
10 9 8 7 6 5 4 3 2 1

Library of Congress Cataloging-in-Publication Data

Names: Orgel, Stephen, author.
Title: The invention of Shakespeare, and other essays /
Stephen Orgel.
Description: 1st edition. | Philadelphia : University of
Pennsylvania Press, [2022] | Includes bibliographical
references and index.
Identifiers: LCCN 2021031920 | ISBN 9780812253740
(hardcover)
Subjects: LCSH: Shakespeare, William, 1564-1616—
Criticism and interpretation. | Shakespeare, William,
1564-1616—Criticism, Textual. | Shakespeare, William,
1564-1616—Dramatic production.
Classification: LCC PR2976 .O74 2022 | DDC 822.3/3—dc23
LC record available at https://lccn.loc.gov/2021031920

For
David Kastan

Contents

Introduction

The underlying theme of all the essays in this collection is what I have called the invention of Shakespeare, the creation of an author suited to the increasing canonicity of the works.[1] Several of the essays share a concern with what we might call glitches in Shakespeare, moments where the text does something unexpected, and that therefore requires explanation, emendation, or some radical inventiveness in editing or in performance. These include things that seem like false starts (Cassio at the beginning of *Othello* is "almost damned in a fair wife" but is thereafter unmarried; Antonio at the beginning of *The Tempest* is said to be accompanied by a "brave son," who never appears) or confusions that seem quite pointless but can hardly be accidental (in *As You Like It* there are two characters named Jaques, and in the *Henry IV* plays two characters named Bardolph); aborted happy endings (such as those in *Love's Labor's Lost* and *Twelfth Night*); and real surprises (the impenitent villains at the happy conclusions of *Much Ado About Nothing* and *The Tempest*; Isabella's silence at the Duke's proposal of marriage at the end of *Measure for Measure*; the fact that, contradicting both the chronicle histories and every other version of the Lear story, Lear and Cordelia lose the final battle and die). Some of these (e.g., Cassio's "fair wife" and Antonio's "brave son") go by so quickly in the theater that audiences are scarcely aware of them; but for the original spectators the endings of *Love's Labor's Lost* and *Twelfth Night* would have been a surprise, or even a disappointment; and the ending of *King Lear*, for anyone who knew British history, would surely have seemed perverse.

These examples are so various that it is difficult to generalize about them, but they are characteristically Shakespearean, not least in the way the editorial and critical tradition has ignored or dismissed them or tried to argue them away. But false starts, second thoughts, confusions, and changes of mind are characteristics of any work in progress, and they do stamp the play not as a finished artifact but as a stage in a process. That is what the text of a play is: we have come to think of a book as something final, achieved; a play, however, is not conceived as a book but as a work for performance, and the performance is based, but only in part, on the text we call a script. The script is not the play, it is only where the play starts. The actors turn it into a play, and every revival of the play—and indeed, every performance—is different. There is never a "final" version.

Nevertheless, if we study drama, most of what we study is necessarily the texts, that is, books. So the first theoretical issue textual editors of drama need to face is what we are doing when we edit the text of a play. In the case of Shakespeare, there is always some underlying claim that we are getting back to "what Shakespeare actually wrote," but obviously that is not true: we clarify, we modernize, we undo muddles, we correct or explain (or explain away) errors, all in the interests of getting a clear, readable, unproblematic text. In short, we produce what we want Shakespeare to have written or think he "must have"—that is, ought to have—written. But one thing we really do know about Shakespeare's original text is that it was hard to read.

"The Desire and Pursuit of the Whole" charts the beginnings of the creation of the monumental Shakespeare, the author not merely of popular poetry and successful plays, but of *Works*. What constituted the works, however, changed from era to era. The first collected edition, the first folio, did not even include all the plays; and though in his own time Shakespeare was best known to the reading public as a poet, it was not until the eighteenth century that the poems were first included in collections claiming to be his complete works. The poems did not invariably remain there until the twentieth century.

"No Sense of an Ending," "The Poetics of Incomprehensibility," "Getting Things Wrong," "Two Household Friends" and "Revising *King Lear*" focus in various ways on the sorts of puzzles I have termed glitches, whether typographical (in the case of "No Sense of an Ending"), grammatical (in "The Poetics of Incomprehensibility"), or discursive. These essays therefore necessarily also constitute histories of editorial ingenuity. They are in addition histories of scholarly credulity: what constitutes a believable explanation changes from era to era, though modern editions of Shakespeare are still heavily indebted to eighteenth-century strategies of elucidation and emendation, the translation (or reduction) of complex poetry into clear, sensible prose.

"Food for Thought" and "Venice at the Globe" were written for particular occasions, the former for a session at a meeting of the Renaissance Society of America on food in Elizabethan culture, the latter for a conference of historians and philosophers in the Veneto, at the University of Padua. "Food for Thought" is about feasting on Shakespeare's stage. Shakespearean dinners often include unpleasant surprises—the surprise, indeed, is usually the point of the meal (as in *The Taming of the Shrew* at the beginning of Shakespeare's career and *The Tempest* at the end of it), a vehicle of outrage and revenge (*Titus Andronicus*), and the background for planning a murder and the setting for its retribution (*Macbeth*). Even in less highly charged situations, food is freighted with ethical implications: Prince Hal deplores the meager proportion of bread to sack in Falstaff's diet, and Hamlet has a similar criticism of dinners at his uncle's court; Shylock refuses to dine with his Venetian clients; King Lear's dinner does not arrive quickly enough. Dramatically, what makes for a satisfactory meal?

"Venice at the Globe" is about the representation of Venice on the Elizabethan and Jacobean stage. Venice in Shakespeare's time was already a popular destination for British gentlemen, renowned for its culture, as well as for its luxury and depravity. It was increasingly important as an artistic center, a supplier of paintings for the growing number of English aristocratic connoisseurs. In Elizabethan political theory, moreover, the Venetian republic was a model for the ideal commonwealth, implicitly a version of England, with its impartial legal system and its Great Council as a parallel to Parliament. In the theater of Shakespeare and Jonson, however, the city was not idealized at all, but was a hotbed of plots, financial danger, and romantic agony. In fact, in the drama, Venice is less a model for England than a mirror reflecting England's fears and vices. Shakespeare and Jonson clearly knew very little about the city: Venice at the Globe was essentially Elizabethan London.

The performing tradition has its own editorial methods, and the two essays on performance discuss four notable productions of Shakespeare plays as interpretive critiques, of both the plays themselves and their traditional presentation on the stage. Productions typically cut plays, in part so as to reduce the performing time (the plays on the Elizabethan stage must also have been cut), but also in order to make texts that, in reading, require a good deal of elucidation into scripts that are accessible to theater audiences, who cannot consult glosses and notes. But the cuts also reveal interpretive assumptions about the plays and about what we want the plays to be. Consider *Hamlet* on the modern stage: in the text, Hamlet is by turns manic and depressed, not a little mad. This is an element of the play that tends to be reduced in modern productions, in the interests of making Hamlet a contemplative philosopher. He *is* a contemplative philosopher, but only intermittently, between bouts of antic disruptiveness; and the disruptive antics really are essential to the play—they are what frightens Claudius about Hamlet, not his philosophical musings. In the famous and notably successful *Hamlet* film of 1948, Laurence Olivier in his opening scenes established the prince as a deeply contemplative figure, a convincing interpretation that, however, depended on the excision of about a third of Hamlet's lines. There is nothing invalid about this—every age produces the Hamlet it wants— nor could we perform an authentically Elizabethan *Hamlet* if we wanted to: to begin with, we would have to create an Elizabethan audience.

But the Italian productions of Shakespeare I attended seemed more genuinely in touch with the plays than anglophone productions often are, particularly with how to update problematic elements so that they worked dramatically and did not disrupt the tone of the whole. Sometimes their theatrical strategies were ones that would simply not be feasible in a British or American production, depending for their success on an audience with fewer, or different, expectations of Shakespeare. Thus, replacing the drunken "cakes and ale" scene in *Twelfth Night* with a little Rossini farce worked brilliantly in Rome, whereas it might be greeted with indignation or bafflement in London.

Danny Scheie's Shakespeare has always elicited excitement and praise but also deep indignation from those for whom any Shakespearean drama is a canonical text. As I say in the essay: "Every production is a selective version of the text, and Scheie's *Tempest* remained deeply in touch with a dimension that

most directors ignore or understate: its essential character as both spectacular
theater and comedy . . . Scheie's *Tempest* was about the possibilities of comic
theater." Scheie's Shakespeare is also always concerned with cultural relevance,
just as in Shakespeare's age theater was a potent vehicle of social commentary,
often deliberately offensive, or assumed to be—hence the pervasive censorship throughout the period (and the censorship of theater in Britain survived
almost until the present). The relevance in modern terms often comes out as
comic—though not invariably: there was a good deal in Scheie's *Cymbeline*
reflecting genuinely frightening elements in Thatcherite Britain—but the hilar-
ity the production elicited was a measure of how genuinely engaged audiences
were by it. Such interpretations are subversions not of the plays but rather of
traditional pieties about the plays, enlightening in the way any good parody is.
Scheie's theatrical strategies are characteristically startling, often disconcerting,
even frankly outrageous; but they have seemed to me more often right than
wrong and have sometimes produced genuine revelations.

As with any collection of essays written over a thirty-year period, these
include occasional inconsistencies, repetitions, and things I have changed my
mind about. I have adjusted the most egregious of these but have not undertaken any major revisions. Dates of composition are indicated at the end of
each essay.

1

The Invention of Shakespeare

I

What happens when a play becomes a book—what is required to make it a book, what function does the book serve, who buys it and why? For readers in his lifetime, Shakespeare was best known as the poet of *Venus and Adonis* and *Lucrece*, which went through many more editions than any of the plays. Before his death in 1616, eighteen of the plays had appeared in quarto, and the plays in quarto look quite different from the versions in the folio, which, with their acts and scenes (however erratically included) and even an occasional cast list, set the standard for the subsequent presentation of a Shakespeare play. One other quarto appeared in 1622, and the publication of the first folio in 1623 added eighteen more. Thus before 1623, people interested in Shakespeare as a dramatist knew half the plays only as recollections of performances.

We tend to assume that the purchasers of play quartos were people who had liked the play in performance and wanted to remember it—reading the text was a way of mentally reconstructing the performance. But there is some significant counterevidence to this point: the early *Hamlet* quartos insert commonplacing marks (marginal quotation marks) to indicate memorable bits: the play is being treated as a repository of excerptable wisdom. Ben Jonson rewrote his own plays for publication, and annotated them, and even claimed that the performances had misrepresented the play—the real play, for Jonson, was not the performance, but the text, and a revised text at that. The book of the play was offered as an unmediated address from the playwright to the reader, dispensing with the actors entirely—ironically in the case of Jonson, whose plays depend so heavily on a group of virtuoso actors.

By the time the publisher Humphrey Moseley issued the Beaumont and Fletcher folio in 1647, Moseley could claim that the texts were the *real* plays: the actors had varied the texts, by cutting, or by adapting them to various circumstances. But the book, Moseley said, contains "all that was spoken and all that was not," "the whole play," "without the least mutilation"—Moseley assumed that what performance does is mutilate the play.[1] One could say that this assumption goes back as far at least as Aristotle, whose treatise on drama is *The Poetics*, not something like "The Theatrics," and the emphasis of the argument is not on performance but on plot. At the same time, though the history of drama has been, necessarily, a history of texts, anyone who has worked in theater knows how much effort is involved in translating the text of a play back into a performance.

Most of what I am calling the invention of Shakespeare has been done by editors, dutifully followed, usually at some distance, by biographers.[2] For all the claims of scientific bibliography, editing has always been more of an art than a science, with the editor more a collaborator than a technician, an enabler, but with ideas about the nature of the finished work that are frequently quite different from those of the author. And for literature in English, literature as an institution, the great originary figures are not Chaucer, Gower, Langland, and least of all the poet of *Beowulf,* nor the scribes or patrons of the often magnificent manuscripts in which these works were preserved, but the first editors and publishers, William Caxton, Richard Pynson, Wynkyn de Worde. Caxton, coming to England to practice the trade he had learned in Burgundy, was the crucial architect of the literary book as we know it in English, the creator of a particular kind of great book, the book as a collection of narratives, and in later ages as a collection of Works, or by the seventeenth century, Plays. For us the most significant of these appeared under the name of an author—Chaucer's *Canterbury Tales*, Malory's *Morte Darthur*, and eventually Ben Jonson's *Workes*, Shakespeare's *Comedies, Histories and Tragedies*—but more often the collection had no name, or only an ambiguous one, attached to it: *The Recuyell of the*

Histories of Troy, Dictes or Sayengis of the Philosophres, The Golden Legend. The author of the work we now know as Higdon's *Polychronicon* identifies himself only as "Ranulph monk of Chestre," but the final words of the volume are "fynysshed per Caxton." The authorizing figure was Caxton himself, whether as author, translator, compiler, editor, printer, or publisher. Such functions were not separate, and most early publisher-printers were involved with all of them. In the case of these early printers, the collection and systemization of manuscripts and the translation of manuscripts into print constituted the inauguration of an English literary canon, with the author very far from the center of the system.

That, at least, is one way of constructing the story. But printers were not always, or even usually, concerned with creating canons. Most of what Caxton, like most printers, produced was ephemeral and entirely marginal to what we mean by literature. The early modern printed book could be a monument, like Caxton's, Pynson's, and de Worde's *Canterbury Tales*, but it could also be, and much more often was, mercurially transient. Ephemera, indeed, were what kept printers in business. While the typesetting slowly proceeded on the masterworks of the beginning of English literature, the same presses were turning out innumerable broadsheets, handbills, pamphlets, decrees, edicts, proclamations, prayers, calendars, indulgences; and a few decades later, they printed ballads, accounts of battles, festivals, funerals, trials, executions, deathbed conversions, and lurid stories of all kinds—these paid the bills. During times of crisis and debate polemical pamphlets filled the bookstalls in huge numbers and were swiftly replaced by the replies they generated. Pamphlets participating in the Lutheran revolution or the English Civil War were especially unstable, full of changes of mind, often sent to the press incomplete, and often attacked or refuted before they were even published. They were also almost instantly outdated—for the publisher, indeed, this was their greatest virtue, their creation of a continuing market for instantaneous refutation. The book in such cases was less a product than a process, part of an ongoing dialectic.

The press was thus the agent both of canonicity and of its opposite, the radical instability of the polemical and occasional. It generated both literature on the one hand, and on the other news, by definition quickly outdated, and publicity, the printed equivalent of the spam that today constitutes most of what fills our virtual libraries and which we almost instantly discard. We are necessarily more aware of the history of the canonical, an awareness that was effectively engineered by the publishers: great books were from the beginning characteristically printed in large expensive volumes designed to survive. This was not, however, on the whole, good business—the books made money, certainly, but cultural capital and prestige are not easily marketable. The first folio of Shakespeare, which appears to us the most foolproof of investments, took ten years to sell out; the second folio took more than thirty years; the third folio took another thirty. Hence the necessity for publishing the endlessly proliferating, culturally all but invisible, eminently marketable, ephemera.

These remained invisible until the mid-seventeenth century, when a single collector, George Thomason, interested in the English revolution as it was being fought out in print, decided to treat the myriad of ephemera as history. For the first time, somebody considered instantly obsolete pamphlets worth collecting and preserving, and thus created a market, and thereby a value, for them, and an archive for us (now preserved as the Thomason Tracts in the British Library). Survival in this case depended on the special tastes of the collector—as it does, in fact, in all cases: it is not printing that effects continuity and promises permanence, but connoisseurship and bibliophily. These are, however, largely irrelevant to the printers' interests, which are precisely in the ephemeral character of their production, the rapidity of its transformation from irresistible to worthless, its almost instant obsolescence. Even the Great Book, the Works of Chaucer, Shakespeare, or Milton, depends for its viability on a continuing market for new editions. What was novel and unique in Thomason's love of books was his extension of connoisseurship to the ephemeral. The innovation was in readers, not publishers: the agent of change was not the press but its audience.

It took many generations for printing to develop norms, and the central and the marginal have always maintained an unstable dialogue. It is the marginal that defines the central, revealing its limits, but where any book lies on that continuum is often clear only in hindsight. The great Venetian publisher Aldus Manutius made his fortune creating the first series of "pocket" classics, the major ancient texts in quarto and octavo aimed at humanist readers. He also undertook to produce a modern classic, the *Hypnerotomachia Poliphili*, a long and abstruse dream vision probably written in the 1460s by a cleric named

Francesco Colonna—this was the first contemporary work printed by Aldus and the first in the vernacular; but its Italian was so convoluted and so heavily Latinate that it was readable only by the most scholarly aficionados—one could hardly call its language a vernacular. On this work Aldus lavished all the art and skill his resources could command: he commissioned an exquisitely elegant new typeface and woodcut illustrations that are among the finest produced in fifteenth-century Italy and printed the book in 1499 in a superbly designed folio on beautiful paper with generous margins. Sales were abysmal; by 1508 most of the edition remained unsold—the edition would have been no more than five hundred copies, but this represented a huge investment. The book was designed to be central, a modern classic, but has remained at the margins of literature, admired but unread, coveted by bibliophiles purely as an art object.

Still, one aspect of the work was not marginal: the integration of text and picture was unparalleled and set a standard for book illustration that can still be seen in book design of the nineteenth and twentieth centuries. Even here, however, the function of the illustrations is ambiguous. They realize things described in the text but they elucidate nothing, and if they have any value at all in the plot, it is only to give some sense of visual context to an otherwise impenetrable narrative—rather as if Matisse had illustrated *Finnegans Wake* instead of *Ulysses*. The illustrations and typography have almost from the beginning constituted the primary attraction of this book. Thus the marginal becomes central.

There are, of course, illustrated books in which the illustrations are not marginal. For many kinds of books they convey information—scientific texts, geographies, iconologies, and iconographies (though the earliest iconographies were not illustrated). In these the pictures may be said to do part of the work of the book; but there are also books in which the illustrations are essential because they constitute not its work but its play, books designed to give pleasure in which the visual element provides much of the pleasure, as it does in the *Hypnerotomachia Poliphili*. Such books extend the long and rich tradition of illuminated manuscripts, with their historiated initials and decorative borders. For the history of printing, the landmark enterprise was the massive *Liber Chronicarum*, or Nuremberg Chronicle, of 1493, an astonishing tour de force in which every page includes woodcut illustrations that maintain a continuous complex visual dialectic with the text. There are portraits of monarchs, biblical figures, legendary heroes, even of God the Father; there are family trees, exotic animals, cosmographical maps, and hundreds of cityscapes. Here again the images only rarely provide information: most of the portraits are necessarily imaginary; a small number of the cityscapes are topographically correct, but for the most part the city views are generic, with the same image typically doing service for several different places. But the relation between text and image remains secure: everything in this text has its visual counterpart, and the integration of typography with woodcut is seamless. The book presents itself as a universal history, but it is also a virtuosic display of the art of printing.

In England, the illustration of books developed haphazardly. English decorative title pages began later than those on the continent and were on the whole, at least initially, less promiscuous. By the first decade of the sixteenth century, English publishers were regularly using title-page illustrations that were directly related to the text; and in the next decade developed decorative borders for their titles. By the middle of the century, they were commissioning elaborate woodcut title pages, and though these were often specific to the books they were prepared for, as in the famous titles for William Cunningham's *Cosmographical Glasse* (1559) and the folio edition of Sidney's *Arcadia* (1593), they were subsequently used indiscriminately for other works to which they had no relevance—the *Cosmographical Glasse* woodcut, for example, designed for a work on cosmography and navigation, in 1560 introduced the *Works* of Thomas Becon, the Protestant divine; in 1564 a commentary on the book of Judges; in 1570 a Euclid; in 1572 a volume on British ecclesiastical antiquities; in 1574 the Acts of King Alfred; and later, Thomas Morley's *Introduction to Practical Music* (1597, 1608), books of ayres by John Dowland (1597, 1600, 1606, 1613) and Philip Rosseter (1601) as well as Sternhold and Hopkins's *Psalms* (1605). In 1604 it was even used for the fourth edition of Sir Philip Sidney's *Arcadia*. In all, it was used as the title page for eighteen different works during more than half a century. Moreover, in the absence of biographies, what readers knew about authors beyond what could be gleaned from the texts was limited to the frontispiece portraits, which began to be standard in large volumes of collected works only in the seventeenth century.

The claim that throughout the incunabular period print was marginal, that there was some stigma attached to print, is still commonly encountered, though it was long ago exploded. It was largely invented by the historian Jacob Burckhardt, who cited an agent of the Duke of Urbino to the effect that his master scorned the products of the new technology. In fact the ducal library was ordering printed books from Roman publishers as early as the 1470s and contained a large number of handsome and expensive ones. The agent's claim was eccentric in the extreme, if not an outright lie; in any case, it was clearly a case of special pleading: its author was in the business of supplying manuscripts. Analogously, it is a commonplace that throughout the English Renaissance the socially degrading aspects of print prevented aristocratic writers from publishing their work. This claim too needs careful scrutiny. Such counterexamples as the Countess of Pembroke's edition of her brother Sir Philip Sidney's writings and her own play *Antonie*, the several publications of the Earl of Stirling, the Earl of Newcastle's plays, not only published but performed in the public theater, Lady Mary Wroth's *Urania*, which she was criticized for but published anyway, the various works of Margaret Cavendish, Duchess of Newcastle, are rarely taken into account. (If the Earl of Oxford had written plays and put his name to them, he would have been in very good company.) What is certainly the case is that print and manuscript culture continued to flourish side by side until late in the seventeenth century. Each had its place. John Donne said he did not want his poems published because he would then be unable to control who read them. He sent particular poems to particular people—friends, lovers, potential patrons—and varied the poems according to their recipients. Some kinds of literature were personal, other kinds public, and these categories could change over time.

It is significant, however, that the assertion of literary authority is almost always referred to manuscript evidence, as the editors of the Shakespeare folio say the book is to be trusted because it is based on "the true original copies," even though the true originals in this case are for the most part not authorial but the scribal copies that constituted the prompt books; whereas several of the Shakespeare quartos, which the folio aims to replace with authoritative texts, do derive directly from Shakespeare's holographs. Editors still regularly make the same sort of claim in reverse—that their revisions and sophistications are returning the text to what the author actually wrote. But this occludes how deeply imbedded the scribe, editor, printer, and publisher all are and have always been in what finally reaches us as the work of literature.

Manuscript is for us marginal, in the sense that the norm of literature is print. We feel that a book has not reached its final form until it exists in type, between covers, in multiple copies. Nevertheless, as I have suggested, for editors the manuscript has always had a curious kind of centrality. When C. H. Herford and Percy and Evelyn Simpson did their great Oxford edition of Ben Jonson, they systematically reproduced manuscript texts when these survived, despite the fact that Jonson saw his own works through the press and made changes in the course of printing. Oxford's printer then had to devise typographical equivalents to Jonson's manuscript conventions, though instead of erasing the distinction between the two, this procedure only emphasized them. But it was the reproduction of the manuscript—or more precisely, the illusion that the manuscript was being reproduced—that was felt to make the edition authoritative.

II

Editing is not a neutral process. It always involves basic decisions that are not dictated by the text but by the editor's attitudes toward the text. How do we want the work to appear? Current practice, obviously market driven, overwhelmingly prefers at least the well-known Renaissance authors to be presented in thoroughly modernized texts—the new Cambridge Ben Jonson, designed to supersede Oxford's Herford and Simpson, has all the scholarly apparatus one could desire, but the texts are in relentlessly modern English (hence there are no "mushrumps" and no "porcpisce," Jonson's versions of the mushroom and porpoise, the latter fancifully etymologized as a pig-fish). Equally modernized, of course, are the texts of practically every Shakespeare currently available.

Scholars typically deplore the situation; but do we really want the work as a historical document, with all its period elements intact? These involve not only old spelling and impressionistic punctuation but typographical conventions that seriously reduce the accessibility of the work—the failure to distinguish i and j, u and v; the long s, so easy to confuse with an f. This particular confusion was common even in the sixteenth and seventeenth centuries: the printer of *Macbeth* has Banquo ask "How farre is't call'd to Soris" (1.3.39).[3] The name of the town is Forres and has been regularly emended to that, generally without comment, in editions since the eighteenth century. But modern editors also invariably retain the name of Macbeth's father in the line "By *Sinells* death, I know I am *Thane* of Glamis" (1.3.71). The historical Macbeth's father's name was Finel, or Finley—this is the same transcription error as that in Soris, apparently deriving from the fact that the two names were not capitalized in the original manuscript, and therefore the initial f could be read as s; to my knowledge only two editors, both very recent (one of them myself), emend the name to correct the error.[4] Why then print Forres but not Finel? Does geography matter while genealogy does not? There is no answer to this question, but it reminds us of the extent to which editing is an art, not a science. Many of its decisions are frankly arbitrary.

The look of the text too is often—perhaps always—more a matter of what we might call aesthetic politics than of any adherence to an original. Merritt Hughes's Milton, the standard edition for university courses for well over half a century, fully and usefully annotated, and with excellent historically informed introductions, presents a text that by any scholarly standards is a sham. It is a fully modernized text that pretends not to be: archaic spellings (though none so archaic as to be confusing) are randomly introduced; Milton's erratic capitalization is erratically observed; the punctuation is not Milton's but neither is it quite modern. In short, this is a text in modern English that has been "antiqued." The text of the Riverside Shakespeare, one of the most admired editions of the past half century, has been similarly antiqued, though less egregiously: G. Blakemore Evans, the textual editor, introduced an occasional archaism, just to give the feel of an old text.

What is the feel of an old text, or rather, what do we want an old text to feel like? W. Carew Hazlitt, writing in the mid-nineteenth century, spoke for an age in which the scholar-editor had not yet replaced the antiquarian when he deplored "ponderous metrical romances . . . reproduced in modern types . . . destitute even of those twin charms, black letter and uniqueness."[5] Hazlitt was celebrating the growth of a "more healthy and discriminating spirit" in the taste for old texts (that is, a spirit that could discriminate between lively old texts and ponderous ones), but he was also decrying the use of black letter type in the presentation of the text, as if a historically informed typography provided merely a specious charm, and only a modern type face would allow the truth of the work to be manifest. The argument has an obvious kind of validity, if one's object is to purge the work of any touch of antiquarianism. But literature is not a platonic idea, independent of its time and culture, and it is independent least of all of its material embodiment. George Herbert's *The Temple* in its 1633 pocket-sized octavo edition is a comforting *vademecum,* whereas in its modern manifestation in the Oxford English Texts it is a massive volume, overwhelmed with its scholarly apparatus.

III

In his own time, Shakespeare was best known to the reading public as a poet. The folio changed all that; and without the folio, half of what we know of Shakespeare would be lost. There would be no *Midsummer Night's Dream, As You Like It, Twelfth Night, Macbeth, Antony and Cleopatra,* or *Coriolanus.* Even after the publication of the folio, in the absence of a biography, our sense of Shakespeare the author would derive only from commendatory verses, occasional reminiscences, the folio title page portrait, and the bust on his monument in Holy Trinity church in Stratford, where he is buried.[6] Decades after his death, when the antiquarian John Aubrey began gathering information for his *Brief Lives,* the biography was meager indeed. Aubrey gives his birthplace correctly but says his father was a butcher (John Shakespeare was a leather worker and glove maker and held a number of important civic positions). Aubrey also claims, on no known authority, that in his youth Shakespeare had been a country schoolmaster and that in his London years he paid annual visits to his family in Stratford. Beyond these, there is nothing in the biography that could be said to constitute information, and nothing about his life in the theater beyond the observation that "his Playes tooke well."[7]

But by the beginning of the eighteenth century enough material had accumulated for the full-scale biography introducing Nicholas Rowe's edition of the plays, published in 1709—the eighteenth century started by creating a life. His marriage, his children, and his move to London were well enough attested, but the "missing years" before he was first recorded as being in London generated an increasingly elaborate set of narratives. Rowe's biography introduces a very circumstantial story of the young Shakespeare's prosecution for poaching deer and his subsequent "escape" to London and the world of the playhouse (Aubrey's country schoolmaster is not part of this narrative). There is no evidence to substantiate this story, and it was over the years replaced with a number of others, equally speculative (for example, that he was a secret Catholic under the name of William Shakeshaft), but it derives, like most of Rowe's biographical detail, from material gathered by the actor Thomas Betterton, who went to Stratford in search of recollections about the poet. The poaching story cannot simply have been invented, but since it concerns events that would have taken place over a century earlier, the possibilities for confusion and error are obviously very great (it may not even have begun as a story about Shakespeare) and it largely disappeared from versions of Shakespeare's life.

An equally unsubstantiated claim of Rowe's, however, has remained firmly within the biographical canon: that he played the Ghost in *Hamlet*. Another story, first recorded in the mid-eighteenth century by the antiquarian William Oldys, has also remained canonical: that Shakespeare played the old man Adam in *As You Like It*. The evidence for this is far more detailed: it was said to be the distant recollection of a younger brother of Shakespeare's when he was a very old man. In fact, none of Shakespeare's three brothers outlived him, but this is another claim about Shakespeare's professional life that has simply been too good to give up. The idea of Shakespeare playing the Ghost who is the source of the plot of *Hamlet* has a kind of symbolic appropriateness, and one can imagine it being invented—*se non è vero è ben trovato*—whereas it is difficult to conceive of the Adam story deriving from nothing but *As You Like It*; but once again, the events concerned are so far in the past that there is no way of determining the truth of the matter, or even if there is any truth at all in it. Both these stories are still regularly cited, with the disclaimer, to be sure, that there is no evidence for them; but they both purport to provide information that we badly want: what roles did Shakespeare write for himself? This is all part of the invention of a biography for Shakespeare.

For most of the eighteenth century the purported remnants of Shakespeare tended to be physical mementos: objects made from the wood of the mulberry tree from Shakespeare's garden, which was cut down in 1750; "Shakespeare's 'Courting Chair'" in Anne Hathaway's cottage near Stratford, carved with the initials W. A. S., for William and Anne Shakespeare, and the Shakespeare coat of arms; and in the mid-nineteenth century, the ultimate remnant, a supposed death mask, revealed in Germany and still on display there. By the end of the eighteenth century the relics started to include documentary and literary items. Those produced by William Henry Ireland are well known—Ireland also "discovered" the wooing chair. His documents included receipts for payments for performances at court, letters to and from the playwright (including an epistolary exchange with Queen Elizabeth), and a love letter to Anne Hathaway enclosing a lock of his hair. Ireland also revealed the manuscripts of two previously unknown plays, *Vortigern* and *Henry II*.

Vortigern was actually produced at Drury Lane in 1796—Richard Brinsley Sheridan, the proprietor, contracted for it as soon as its existence was announced, before anyone had read it. Today, it seems an obvious, preposterous pastiche, but it was initially credible enough for John Philip Kemble, Sarah Siddons, and the popular Dorothea Jordan to agree to be the leads. Siddons dropped out only a week before the opening—from her correspondence it is clear that she recognized the play as a fake. Jordan and Kemble remained in the cast, but Kemble ensured the play's failure by repeating an unfortunate line of Vortigern's, "And when this solemn mockery is o'er," which the audience found hilarious. There was no subsequent performance. Interestingly, the playbill makes no mention of Shakespeare but calls it simply a new play never acted, which certainly was accurate. Since the work's only attraction would have been Shakespeare's name, it is clear that by the opening night even the Drury Lane management had their doubts.

The Ireland papers were so quickly exposed and acknowledged that they have entered into the historical record only as an index to the extent of the mania for Shakespeare, rather than (like the stories about what roles he took in his own plays) as part of what we think we know about him. John Payne Collier's inventions were more subtle and have been especially difficult to expose partly because Collier was a genuinely good scholar and knew what the evidence ought to look like, but even more because he created information that we have badly wanted to be true. One of the most striking and pernicious, if it is a forgery (as seems probable, but the case is not absolutely clear), is the story of amateur performances of *Hamlet* and *Richard II* on a merchant ship anchored off the coast of Sierra Leone in 1607–1608. These purport to be entries in the diary of William Keeling, captain of a ship called the *Dragon*, or sometimes the *Red Dragon*. The diary entries were suspect from the beginning, and not only because they are too good to be true. They do not appear in the first published edition of Keeling's diary, in Samuel Purchas's *Purchas His Pilgrimes*, 1625, and the original manuscript volume that should have included them had disappeared from the East India Company Library by the mid-nineteenth century, when the entries were first described and people undertook to check them. Sidney Lee in his *Life of Shakespeare* (1898) firmly declared the entries spurious,[8] but they continued to be part of the record—if they are too good to be true, they are also too good to abandon. In 2011 Bernice Kliman assembled a good deal of evidence to argue cogently that they were a Collier forgery; in 2018, Richmond Barbour and Bernhard Klein, judiciously weighing Kliman's arguments, concluded that the surviving evidence in fact does not allow us to determine whether the diary entries are forgeries or not—Barbour and Klein focus instead on their significance in the construction of the modern Shakespeare.[9]

From our perspective, the most suspicious thing about the entries is precisely Shakespeare's presence in them. If Collier invented these performances, he did so because he perceived that the monumental Shakespeare constructed over the previous century was really a gigantic anachronism. If it could be shown that during Shakespeare's lifetime his plays were being performed on ships sailing around the world, he would already have been the international phenomenon he ultimately became. The diary entries would then justify the Shakespeare of Collier's own age, the Shakespeare of Coleridge, the Kembles, Edmund Kean, Hazlitt, the Lambs, by refashioning the Shakespeare of 1608.

In fact, throughout the seventeenth century, there were widespread performances of English plays on the continent and even farther afield, by both peripatetic English comedians and native actors: the essential work has been done by Jerzy Limon and Anston Bosman.[10] This work has not really been taken into account. The trouble with it, for bardolators, is that very few of the plays were by Shakespeare: most were composed of excerpted comic routines that required little or no translation. Of plays still recognizable, the most notable is a number of versions of Marlowe's *Doctor Faustus*. But the greatest international success by far was the anonymous play *Nobody and Somebody*, performed first by traveling English companies and then by Dutch comedians, who even went to the Far East with the Dutch East India Company, where the play was so famous that the two central characters, Nobody and Somebody, were produced as figurines in Delft and exported and sold in Asia. This is what we want *Hamlet* to have been; but the most nearly universal English play, the true multicultural phenomenon, was a comedy we care nothing about, a play that scarcely makes it into the histories of English drama.

As for Shakespeare, *Romeo and Juliet* appears in several German lists, *Titus Andronicus* and *King Lear* each in one, and there are several references to *Jew of Venice* plays, which may or may not derive from Shakespeare—the Jew, when named, is named Joseph. But as far as the evidence will take us, *Hamlet* outside England was represented by the German *Der Bestrafte Brüdermord*, *Fratricide Punished*, which must have been based at least partly on the version of the play in the first quarto (the Polonius figure is named Corambus)—in short, not at all the *Hamlet* we want, if this peripatetic play is to represent the historical Shakespeare famous throughout the world in his own time.

If the journal entries are fictitious (as seems to me likely), Collier was not simply revising history; he was inventing it, because it was only in the nineteenth century that *Hamlet* became the quintessential, iconic Shakespeare play. Voltaire had notoriously dismissed it as crude and barbarous—this naturally generated outrage in England, but critics took it seriously enough to spend a good deal of energy refuting it. Samuel Johnson, however, had been scarcely less pejorative, skeptical and condescending, and had declared the drama seriously implausible. It was in response to such attitudes that Coleridge wrote his furious denunciation of his critical predecessors and transformed the whole basis of Shakespeare criticism by proclaiming *Hamlet* Shakespeare's deepest expression of *himself*—to declare *Hamlet* implausible was to accuse Shakespeare of not knowing himself. Negative criticism of the play was thus no longer an evaluation of dramatic strategy and an assessment of its success but an *ad hominem* attack on England's greatest literary genius.[11]

In short, *Hamlet* might have been a possible shipboard entertainment in 1828 but not in 1608. During Shakespeare's lifetime, his most popular plays on the stage were *Titus Andronicus* and *Pericles*. *Pericles* only entered the scholarly canon in the late eighteenth century, and critics well into the twentieth century spent a good deal of energy trying to get *Titus* out of it. *Hamlet* as the touchstone for Shakespeare is a modern phenomenon: Collier was following Coleridge, rewriting critical history. Why, then, did he add *Richard II* to the story? Probably because the play appeared, along with *Richard III* and the first part of *Henry IV* in the largest number of published editions during Shakespeare's lifetime. Those were the most popular plays *for readers*; and in that sense the forger's choice of *Richard II* is less anachronistic than the choice of *Hamlet*, though it also indicates an anachronistic reliance on printed texts to determine theatrical popularity.

IV

There is another kind of forgery relating to Shakespeare, which is entirely accepted and even passes unnoticed as simply part of the editorial process: the practice of emendation and elucidation. The essay "Getting Things Wrong" in this volume considers a number of standard emendations, the most famous of which is Lewis Theobald's revision of Mistress Quickly's baffling phrase in her account of Falstaff's death "and a table of green fields" to "and a [i.e., he] babbled of green fields."[12] This emendation was treated as a revelation; and though the problems with it are manifold and have become increasingly clear (see the essay "Getting Things Wrong" in this volume), it did seem not only to have restored a lost original but in a sense to have cracked a code.

But every crux generates a proliferating set of narratives, and there are hidden narratives within every text. Every emendation is a forgery, in the sense that it purports to represent Shakespeare's lost original. This is true even when the emendation is not dubious in the way "a babbled of green fields" is; even when, we would say, the change is obviously correct—as when King Lear says in the quarto, "A dogge, so bade in office," which reads in the folio, "A Dogg's obey'd in Office," and all editors, even those basing their texts firmly on the quarto, follow the folio text.[13] This is, no doubt, a practical solution to an intractable problem, but it ignores all the things we really do not know about Shakespeare's original texts. What does the difference in the two texts signify? It is perfectly possible that Shakespeare's handwriting was sufficiently difficult and his spelling sufficiently eccentric that what the quarto's compositor read as "A dog so bade in office" was actually intended to be read as "A dog's obeyed in office"; but can that simply be assumed? And if so, doesn't every printed line based on a Shakespeare manuscript contain any number of alternative possibilities? Then by correcting the quarto reading we have not restored Shakespeare's lost original; on the contrary, we have emended away the ambiguity and confusion that confronted Shakespeare's original readers—emended away something essential to Shakespeare, produced what he intended to write, or wanted to write, or ought to have written; produced, in short, what we want him to have written.[14]

This is not a modern phenomenon, though it has certainly become increasingly institutionalized in editorial practice since the early eighteenth century; and it is now practically unavoidable, since Shakespeare is big business, and every Shakespeare edition, to find purchasers, has to be modernized. But ever since the earliest edited versions, we have wanted a "correct" Shakespeare, even if Shakespeare's original was not correct. The second folio, published in 1632, is for the most part a page-for-page reprint of the first, preserving even errors in pagination. But it corrects mistakes in Holofernes's Latin in *Love's Labor's Lost*. What is being corrected there? Are these Shakespeare's mistakes, or the mistakes of the scribe who prepared the play for the press, or those of the first compositor incorrectly transcribing a correct manuscript? Or are the mistakes perfectly correct, and is the point that Holofernes's Latin is at fault?

What we have meant by "Shakespeare" has changed with every era. Shakespeare the poet was the essential Shakespeare for his earliest readers, but from the Restoration on, the marketable Shakespeare was Shakespeare the playwright, and the poems increasingly became an afterthought in the construction of his career—most "complete" Shakespeares, until the twentieth century, did not even include the poems. The narrative poems fell out of fashion, and the sonnets had survived only through the heterosexualized versions of John Benson's 1640 edition (Benson changed the gender of pronouns in crucial love poems and supplied titles that established the beloved as a woman)—this was the text Charles Gildon used in the volume of poems appended to the 1709 collected Shakespeare edited by Nicholas Rowe, and it went on being reprinted well into the nineteenth century. Edmond Malone's return to the 1609 text in 1780 met with critical indignation: the age had a great deal invested in a normatively manly Shakespeare, but the original Sonnets presented a Shakespeare in love with another man and committing adultery with a married woman. At the same time, Malone's incorporation of *Pericles* into the canon supplied the idea of Shakespeare with an element of transcendent romance, a necessary attribute for an arch-poet. A century later Edward Dowden was to add Romance as a category of the late Shakespeare, who was no longer to be limited to the mundane genres of Comedy, History and Tragedy.

—(2017/2020)

2

The Desire and Pursuit of the Whole

Although in his own age Shakespeare was much better known to the literate public as a poet than as a playwright, the canonical collection of his works in the seventeenth century, preserved in the first four folios, included only plays. The sole attempt at a comprehensive collection of his poems, published by John Benson in 1640, left the most celebrated poems, *Venus and Adonis* and *Lucrece,* intact but radically readjusted the sonnets, adding titles and combining individual poems, to give the sequence the look of a collection of Cavalier love lyrics and, most notoriously, to transform the beloved young man into a woman. The volume in fact was a miscellany, since it also included a good deal that is not by Shakespeare and is not claimed to be. The first folio itself would not, even in its own time, have been called "complete," since it omitted the very popular *Pericles,* along with the ghostly *Love's Labor's Won* (which must have existed—there are two contemporary references to it,[1] and *Love's Labor's Lost* clearly implies a sequel)—and the collaborative play *The Two Noble Kinsmen* (and the now lost *Cardenio,* which there is no reason to believe had anything to do with Shakespeare),[2] though the presumably collaborative *Henry VIII,* the certainly collaborative *Henry VI* Parts 1 and 2, and *Macbeth* with its additional material by Middleton are included. In 1623 comprehensiveness did not imply completeness. Nor did it in 1632 or 1663, with the publication of the second and third folios, which were basically reprints of the first.

A second issue of the third folio in 1664, however, revealed that the previous folios had not been as comprehensive as they might have been: seven additional plays, including *Pericles*, were added to the canon, all of which had been credited to Shakespeare in his lifetime. If the implications of the first folio had been that this volume contained everything the King's Men considered authentic (or perhaps only everything they owned the rights to, hence not the poems), the implications of the 1664 volume were that more Shakespeare was better Shakespeare, and the adjudication of authenticity was not the business of the publishers.

The enlarged Shakespeare of the third and fourth folios was accepted as the complete Shakespeare by Nicholas Rowe when he produced his edition of the plays in six volumes in 1709, published by Jacob Tonson. The seven additional plays were still grouped together, but they were unambiguously Shakespeare. A year later, as an afterthought, Tonson issued a seventh volume devoted to the poems, with an introduction by Charles Gildon. This was hardly an edition, since it simply reproduced the text of Benson's 1640 *Poems*, with all its revisions; but it did make of Tonson's Shakespeare the first that could be claimed to be in any sense complete. That completeness was quickly declared spurious: Alexander Pope's edition of 1725 banished the seven plays of 1664 and found evidence of collaboration or adulteration throughout the original canon. Adulteration was apparently no problem in the case of the poems, however, which, still in the texts of Benson, were included in an additional volume. The seven plays promptly reappeared in Pope's second edition of 1728, not through any change of heart on Pope's part, but thanks rather to Tonson's conviction that more Shakespeare would sell more copies, and in the hope that some purchasers of the Complete Shakespeare might be willing to replace it with a More Complete Shakespeare. Theobald's and Hanmer's editions of 1733 and 1744 again banished the 1664 plays but also omitted the poems, even though both claimed to represent *The Works of Shakespeare*. *Pericles* was restored to the canon by Edmond Malone in 1780, where it has remained ever since—clearly there was something in *Pericles* that the idea of Shakespeare now could not do without. As for the poems, though Malone abandoned Benson's 1640 volume and returned, more or less, to the texts of the original editions, this did not earn them a place in the canon. George Steevens, appalled by the Shakespeare revealed in Malone's versions of the sonnets—a Shakespeare in love with a young man; a Shakespeare full of lust and committing adultery with a promiscuous married woman—declared that "the strongest act of Parliament that could be framed, would fail to compel readers into their service" [3] and refused them a place in his Shakespeare of 1790—the case was that of *Pericles* in reverse: the sonnets now represented something that the idea of Shakespeare could not tolerate. Though the poems appeared occasionally in the nineteenth century among the Complete Works (for example, in Charles Knight's massive *Pictorial Shakespeare* of 1843 as an addendum to the second volume of Tragedies) it was not until well into the twentieth century that their inclusion as part of the Works became routine; and indeed, Benson's 1640 volume, with its tactfully adjusted versions of Shakespeare's sexuality, was still being reprinted in the mid-nineteenth century.

Meanwhile *The Two Noble Kinsmen* languished in editions of Beaumont and Fletcher throughout the seventeenth and eighteenth centuries, only finally making its appearance as a part of the Shakespeare canon in the second edition of Charles Knight's *Pictorial Shakespeare* of 1866. It has not invariably remained there. When A. R. Braunmuller and I were editing the New Pelican Shakespeare, we proposed including it, and the publisher, having checked the sales figures for the play in the English Penguin series, and finding them far down in the double digits, firmly refused: it attracts fewer readers than even the *Henry VI* plays, which, along with the volume of narrative poems, are the low sellers in our Pelican series. Despite its impeccable credentials, despite the inclusion of other collaborative works in the canon, it has never established itself in the popular mind as Shakespeare. Collected editions that do include the play do so precisely in the interests of a higher completeness—the Riverside edition also includes the Hand D fragment of *Sir Thomas More* and for a moment or two included the notorious *Elegy for William Petre*, eager to be the first Complete Shakespeare that was the most complete. The Oxford Shakespeare goes so far as to provide a précis for the lost *Cardenio*, invented out of its presumed source in *Don Quixote* and Lewis Theobald's *Double Falsehood*, which he claimed to have based on a manuscript of the play he had found. As for the non-dramatic poetry, Colin Burrow's Oxford *Complete Poems* is more than complete, since it includes non-Shakespearean poems ascribed to Shakespeare in his lifetime.

But even when we have the Really Complete Works, how complete are the plays and poems themselves? Surely the impulse to conflate quarto and folio texts of *King Lear, Hamlet, The Merry Wives of Windsor*, and *Romeo and Juliet* springs from a conviction that none of the individual texts is complete. *Macbeth* is obviously incomplete, indicating several of its witches' songs only as incipits ("'Come away, come away' &c.," "'Black spirits' &c."). Some plays actually make a point of not being complete by not completing their action. *Twelfth Night* declares its happy ending deferred until the enraged Malvolio can be mollified, the sea-captain he has had imprisoned released, and Viola's women's clothes restored to her, all of which, if they are presumed to take place at all, will have to do so in another play. *Love's Labor's Lost* explicitly demands a sequel to conclude its suspended wooings. At the end of *The Tempest* Prospero announces his intention of continuing his story outside the limits of the drama, and *All's Well That Ends Well* ends with the ambiguous observation that "All yet seems well," the clear implication being that only time—a time beyond the play—will tell. As for the poems, the several narratives of the sonnets are notoriously, maddeningly incomplete, withholding the name of the beloved youth whose name is to be celebrated for eternity, concealing the identity of the dark mistress, and identifying the rival and the mistress's husband only with the least specific of the poet's own names, Will. The anomalous Sonnet 126 might stand as emblematic of the whole: it consists of twelve lines of the couplets that constitute every other sonnet's end, followed by two sets of empty parentheses, as if to say that the one more couplet that might really do the trick, finally provide some sense of closure, is missing.[4]

Shakespeare's lacunae became a particular problem when the plays started to be conceived as history and productions sought for an archeological correctness. In such an enterprise, consistency and thoroughness are paramount, and these often had to be added to the texts. It is both ironic and characteristic that the first Shakespeare production to claim serious historical credentials should have been Charles Kemble's 1823 *King John*. The play was furnished with settings and costumes based on the scholarly research of James Robinson Planché, and Kemble's playbill included an essay insisting on the historical correctness of this recreation of the past. The scrupulousness was, however, in the service of a history of the reign of King John that does not mention the Magna Carta. Kemble apologized in his playbill for Shakespeare's omission, though, like Macready and Charles Kean after him, he stopped short of rectifying it. Herbert Beerbohm Tree, in his 1899 production of the play, finally supplied the lacuna with a sumptuous pantomime of the king signing the elusive document.

In 1859 Charles Kean presented an elaborate *Henry V* at the Princess's Theatre in London, the culmination of a long series of historical extravaganzas. Here, too, Shakespeare's text was not sufficiently historical for Kean, and he included a number of spectacular reconstructions of events and places that are only described or alluded to in the play, or, in some cases, that are not in the play at all but only in the chronicles on which the play is based—just what he and Macready and Kemble had resisted doing with the Magna Carta in their productions of *King John*. The most lavish of the historical spectacles was devised for Henry's triumphant return to London after the victory at Agincourt, an event that is dispatched in ten lines of the Chorus's prologue to Act 5. In the physical, staged presence of Henry and his army, Kean reasonably enough found the Chorus redundant and cut the ten lines to five, so that his *Henry V* was both more and less complete than Shakespeare's text. Kean's and Tree's mute addenda did more than "correct" Shakespeare; they acknowledged the fact that Shakespeare's concerns often simply do not coincide with ours. Such scenes thus rectify not only history but Shakespeare's imagination as well; but they also confront us with the question of what the real play is, and of what we mean by "Shakespeare."

The problems begin, however, with the very idea of construing drama as history and history as drama, the notion that we can understand the forces that led to the deposition of Richard II, the Wars of the Roses, the Tudor revolution, by inventing dialogue for a few figures mentioned in the chronicles and putting them in dramatic situations. The problem with this assumption is not that it is absurdly reductive: all history, as it undertakes to give a coherent interpretation of the past, is reductive. The problem is what it implies about drama: the logical corollary is that the reality of drama is not what it presents but what is represented in it, the world of fact, behind the text, which the play purports to bring to life—the true history of King John or Henry V, or, for that matter, Hamlet, Prospero: not Shakespeare's poetry, but what really happened. But if drama has become transparent, a glass through which we perceive the real, it is therefore logically subject to any amount of revision to bring it into closer coincidence with that putative reality—hence Kean's historical interludes and Beerbohm Tree's Magna Carta scene, designed to rectify Shakespeare's omissions.

Nor was it only historical lacunae that increasingly required amendment. In Jean-François Ducis's magnificent Racinian *Hamlet* of 1769, Hamlet finally, in Act 5, confronts his mother with the essential question he neglects to ask in Shakespeare, in a scene Shakespeare neglected to write: he demands that she swear, on an urn containing his father's ashes, that she was not complicit in her husband's murder. This was a scene that, even in Shakespeare's own time, was felt to be missing: the first quarto of *Hamlet* adds a conversation between the queen and Horatio in which she finally asserts her innocence. In Ducis's version, however, Hamlet already knows that this is not the case: the Ghost has told him that it was in fact she who administered the poison, though the plot was devised by Claudius. She avoids adding perjury to murder by fainting, and when she revives, Hamlet, oddly, forgives her, observing that however great her crime is, heaven's mercy is greater. Claudius arrives with soldiers to arrest Hamlet, followed immediately by Horatio (here renamed Norceste) leading a mob of Hamlet's supporters and shouting, in the best revolutionary fashion, "Peuple, sauvez Hamlet!" Claudius is dispatched promptly, the queen resolves her own problems by committing suicide, and Hamlet survives to rule happily over the Danes. Despite the availability of two reasonably accurate eighteenth-century translations of the play, this was the version of *Hamlet* that, for almost a century, was performed in France, and it was the version in which Talma's famous Hamlet became famous.

The play has often been felt to be incomplete, despite its immense length. Hamlet is often claimed to be the first dramatic character with an inner life, a genuine psychology, and he certainly claims, in his soliloquies, to have one. Nevertheless, we have argued for centuries about his motivations: that crucial bit of his psychology is missing. To provide motivation became increasingly the task of the actor, in search of a psychologically credible character; and since the psychologically credible changes from age to age, Hamlet has been the most mercurial of figures. Garrick notoriously employed a pneumatic wig for his first sight of the Ghost, so that his hair could stand on end. The lines required this additional bit of business, which was considered sensationally realistic at the time—today it would be a joke. In contrast, Laurence Olivier's beautiful 1948 film presented a melancholy and contemplative Hamlet in his first scene at court, a psychologically consistent and entirely persuasive character. It depended, however, on the excision of about a third of Hamlet's lines in the scene—completeness here was the enemy of credibility.

Editions aspire to completeness through their inclusion of textual variants, as if a textual history of Shakespeare were anything more than a history of departures from a lost original. In the case of Shakespeare, the play as a book is always more complete than the play as a performance, because of the inevitable cutting required to fit the drama into the two, or three and a half, or, in the case of some Victorian spectacles, almost five hours' traffic of the stage over various eras—in the marathon productions of Charles Kean, much of the time was taken up with scenic machinery and with the long pauses necessary for changing the complex sets; so the London *Times* observed about Kean's four-hour *Tempest* that "as for the acting, there is not very much room for it."[5] But one way of "completing" the plays is precisely by transforming them into books, with their introductions and commentary and apparatus that undertake to fill in all the gaps and adjudicate among all the possible alternatives.

Hamlet was refigured through an idea of comprehensiveness into the most monumental book of the twentieth century. The Cranach Press *Hamlet* was published in a German edition in 1929 and in an English edition in 1930.[6] For this tremendously ambitious project, the publisher Count Harry Kessler commissioned a new type based on a font used in the Mainz Psalter of 1457. Edward Gordon Craig was engaged to produce illustrative woodcuts; the book was printed in a strictly limited edition on handmade paper, with a few copies also on vellum.

In 1910 Craig had collaborated with Stanislavsky on a *Hamlet* for the Moscow Art Theatre. For this he designed a non-realistic stage, the central element of which was a set of complex, moveable screens. The collaboration was, from the outset, not a success—Craig's abstract theatre was the wrong vehicle for Stanislavsky's intensely psychologized, character-centered view of drama; moreover, the screens did not work properly and kept falling down. But the concept remained with Craig, and the stage he could not create for Stanislavsky he realized in large measure for Kessler.

Kessler's conception was to present *Hamlet* in a Renaissance setting; the book would be a reflection of the historical *Hamlet*—not, however, the *Hamlet* of the quartos, or the Shakespeare folio, and least of all the putative "real" Hamlet, but a bibliographic embodiment of the towering monument to Renaissance culture that *Hamlet* had become—it would complete the *idea* of *Hamlet*. So the models for the book were the masterpieces of the great fifteenth- and sixteenth-century presses: the Nuremberg Chronicle, the *Hypnerotomachia Poliphili*, the Gutenberg and Koberger bibles, the great Estienne and Plantin editions of the classics. It is significant that Kessler's typeface was based not on a font from Shakespeare's age but on the grandest of the early German models: this Hamlet was the German intellectual, the Wittenburg student, the humanist philosopher and scholar. The design of the book was that of a very grand late fifteenth- or early sixteenth-century scholarly edition: the text was in the center of the page, and in the margins around it, in smaller type, related material was placed. In sixteenth-century editions, the marginal material would have consisted of commentary and notes; Kessler's marginalia were the play's main sources, the Hamlet story in the Latin chronicle of Saxo Grammaticus and the *Histoires Tragiques* of François de Belleforest—these were printed in both the original languages and in translation. For the German edition, the text was the standard translation of Schlegel, embellished by Gerhardt Hauptmann, who supplied several additional scenes (such as the reception of Claudius's emissaries Voltimand and Cornelius by the Norwegian king) to fill in what he conceived to be gaps in the plot and thereby render the play more "complete" than the original. (Schlegel's version itself was not unproblematic: for example, it moves the "To be or not to be" soliloquy to the fifth act.) For the English edition, J. Dover Wilson prepared a more straightforward text based on the second quarto—not, significantly, a conflation of the quarto and folio, which regularly constituted the "complete" English text in the period.

Craig provided seventy-two woodcuts for the German edition and five additional ones for the English version. The deployment of these on the page resembles more the format of the Nuremberg Chronicle than any illustrated scholarly edition of drama: the images are not contained by the typography but are in a full partnership with it, and sometimes seem even in control. (Figure 1) Hamlet and Horatio await the ghost, dwarfed by a setting composed

DIE TRAGISCHE GESCHICHTE VON
DIE TERRASSE

Ham. Die luft gebt scharf, es ist entsetzlich kalt.
Hor. 's ist eine schneidende und strenge luft.
Ham. Was ist die uhr?
Hor. Ich denke, nah an zwölf.
Mar. Nicht doch, es hat geschlagen.
Hor. Wirklich schon?
      Ich hört es nicht. So rückt heran die stunde,
      Worin der geist gewohnt ist, umzugehn.
      Trompetenstoß und geschütz abgefeuert hinter der szene.
      Was stellt das vor, mein prinz?
Ham. Der könig wacht die nacht durch, zecht vollauf,
      Hält schmaus und taumelt den geräuschgen walzer.
      Und wie er züge rheinweins niedergießt,
      Verkünden schmetternd pauken und trompeten
      Den ausgebrachten trunk.
Hor. Ist das gebrauch?
Ham. Nun freilich wohl.
      Doch meines dünkens (bin ich eingeboren
      Und drin erzogen schon) ist's ein gebrauch,
      Wovon der bruch mehr ehrt, als die befolgung.
      Dies schwindelköpfge zechen macht verrufen
      Bei andern völkern uns in ost und west;
      Man heißt uns säufer, hängt an unsre namen
      Ein schmutzig beiwort; und fürwahr, es nimmt
      Von unsern taten, noch so groß verrichtet,
      Den kern und ausbund unsres wertes weg.

                    Der geist kommt.

AUS DES SAXO GRAMMATICUS DÆNISCHER
GESCHICHTE. DRITTES BUCH. ÜBERSETZUNG
der auf seite vier bis zehn wiedergegebenen auszüge.
Horwendil und Fengo, die söhne Gerwendils, wurden
von Rorik, könig von Dänemark, an ihres verstorbenen
vaters stelle zu statthaltern über Jütland gesetzt. Nach

28

Figure 1. Hamlet and Horatio await the Ghost, from *Die tragische Geschichte von Hamlet, Prinzen von Dænemark* (Weimar: Cranach Presse, 1929), with illustrations by Edward Gordon Craig. The running heads are printed in red. Folger Shakespeare Library. Reproduced by permission of the Edward Gordon Craig Estate.

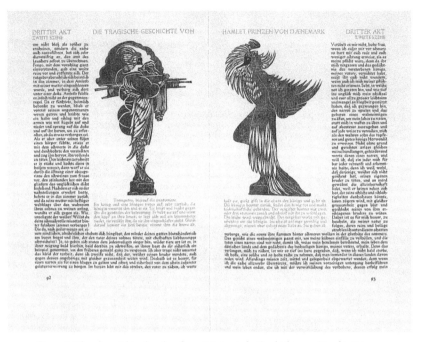

Figure 2. The play within the play, from *Die tragische Geschichte von Hamlet, Prinzen von Dænemark* (Weimar: Cranach Presse, 1929), with illustrations by Edward Gordon Craig. The description of the play and the running heads are printed in red. Folger Shakespeare Library. Reproduced by permission of the Edward Gordon Craig Estate.

of a combination of Craig's woodcut screens, Shakespeare's text, and Saxo's chronicle. Throughout the book, Craig's images are superbly attuned to the play's changes of mood. Several of the woodcuts had to be printed in two stages, to register lighter and darker blacks. For the play scene, a cast of commedia dell'arte characters in black silhouette appears in various formats—freestanding across the bottom margin, within whole scenes incised with white on black and grey backgrounds, in a tiny roundel in the center of a page, and most startling, for the Dumb Show (Figure 2), two elaborately masked and costumed silhouettes replace the central text on two facing pages, with the description of the pantomime printed in red beneath them. Ophelia's last appearance is as a tiny white waiflike form within a grid of pale blue flanked by two of Craig's massive black woodcut screens, with a silhouetted mob beyond them—this is the only use of color in the woodcuts and it is tremendously affecting. There is no illustrated Shakespeare in which the images are so thoroughly integrated with the typography and in which text, book, and performance are conceived so completely as a whole. The Cranach Press *Hamlet* undertakes to rethink the relation of drama, book, and image—in short, the nature of dramatic representation on the page—and from the beginning reconceives the book of the play as a performance and completes the play as a book.

—(2006)

3

No Sense of an Ending

I begin with a few examples of concluding couplets in pre-Shakespearean sonnets:

And graven with diamonds, in letters plain
There is written her fair neck round about
Noli me tangere, for Caesar's I am,
And wild for to hold though I seem tame. (Wyatt)[1]

Such is the power of love in gentle mind,
    That it can alter all the course of kind. (Spenser)[2]

And, not content to be Perfection's heir
Thyself, dost strive all minds that way to move
Who mark in thee what is in thee most fair.
So while thy beauty draws the heart to love,
    As fast that virtue bends that love to good.
    But ah, Desire still cries, Give me some food. (Sidney)[3]

Thus great with child to speak, and helpless in my throes,
    Biting my truant pen, beating myself for spite:
    Fool said my muse to me, look in thy heart and write. (Sidney)[4]

True that on earth we are but pilgrims made,
   And should in soul, up to our country move:
True and yet true, that I must Stella love. (Sidney)[5]

In these examples, the couplet may be part of the sestet, as in the Wyatt sonnet; or it may be a summary of the poem, as in Spenser; or, most interestingly, it may not be a unit at all: in the Sidney sonnets, the first line concludes the movement of the preceding twelve, and the second line reverses or contradicts that movement. The characteristically Shakespearean use of the couplet, to cut off the poem and conclude with a sharp, even cynical, epigram, may be an extension of Sidney's usage, but it differs significantly in treating the couplet definitively as a unit. The tradition of setting the couplet off from the rest of the poem typographically does not begin till the 1590s (as the Spenser example indicates, it was not standard even then), and in relation to the movement of the poem, it makes better sense in Shakespeare than in Sidney.

I turn now to the most striking Shakespearean example, the entirely notional couplet concluding Sonnet 126, a twelve line poem followed by two empty italic parentheses, indicating, at first glance, a missing couplet. The poem itself is problematic, but I begin with the parentheses: what are parentheses? what might a couplet of empty parentheses signify? According to Malcolm Parkes's history of punctuation, parentheses or brackets were "developed in the late fourteenth century to enclose a parenthesis or interpolated matter."[6] They were used from the beginning for any brief interpolation within a syntactically complete period—Ben Jonson, in *The English Grammar*, considers them a form of comma. The use of empty parentheses to indicate something missing or notional is obviously unrelated to this usage, and when I began writing this essay I realized that, so far as I knew, it was unparalleled in the period. I have not found any other examples before the present: modern bibliographical practice in the transcription of documents sometimes uses empty parentheses or brackets to indicate a missing letter or word, but this does not seem to be based on any historical precedent. At this point I became cautious and consulted my friend the omniscient bibliologue Randall McLeod: had he ever seen anything like it? He had not and proceeded both to account for the problem and to complicate it. He pointed out that the 1609 *Sonnets* was set

Figure 3. Shake-speares Sonnets (1609), sigs. H2ᵛ–H3ʳ in reverse, as they would have appeared to the typesetter. Folger Shakespeare Library.

not page by page but by printing formes,[7] so that the compositor would have had before him two pages of poems facing each other. The page with Sonnet 126 is signed H3; it faces the verso of H2, and these two constituted half the forme. Here is what the compositor would have seen (Figure 3).

Thus Sonnet 126 would simply have looked wrong, obviously shorter than the two poems opposite. And though compositors were surely quite used to reading backwards, the sense of the poem would have had nothing to do with their response. (The fifteen-line Sonnet 99 is much less obviously disproportionate in relation to the page opposite.) The parentheses might then have been placed in the forme simply as a marker—possibly on the assumption that two more lines would be supplied before the type was distributed, but equally possible is that they were included simply to indicate that the printer understood that the poem was an anomaly. In that case, the parentheses would have been inserted not to indicate that there was a mistake, something missing, but just the opposite: as an assurance that the lacuna was correct, that something one would have expected to be there was *correctly* not there.

It is unlikely that the compositor intended the parentheses to mean that the poem was incomplete: this is not how parentheses were used. Ellipses are usually signaled by a long dash or a row of dots, as in Ben Jonson's *Epistle to the Countess of Rutland* (*Forest* XII), which in the 1616 folio breaks off in this way:

> Moodes, which the god-like Sydney oft did proue,
> And your braue friend, and mine, so well did loue.
> Who wheresoere he be. . . . .
> *The rest is lost*

Where a longer section of a work is missing, as after the second sestiad of Edward Blount's edition of the 1598 *Hero and Leander*, the ellipsis is indicated by the words *Desunt nonnulla* ("some is missing") or even, as in the three lost sections of Jonson's poetic sequence *Eupheme*, by an apologetic explanation. The 1590 edition of Sidney's *Arcadia*, however, simply breaks off in the middle of a sentence (Figure 4).

The book ends without even an ellipsis—all that is concluded here is the parenthesis. The three asterisks centered on the page several lines below may be intended to stand for the unwritten hundreds of pages of text, but they may just as well be simply a typographic ornament to mitigate the large amount of empty space between the end of the text and the woodblock ornament.

Three asterisks are used once earlier in the book, after the lovesick Amphialus recounts a dream in verse to his beloved Philoclea (Figure 5). It is not clear what the asterisks signify here, but they do not seem to indicate any missing text. What comes before them is an incomplete sentence, but if that is the point they ought to precede the period, not follow it. They seem more like a dramatic pause, as Amphialus waits in vain for the response to his performance. There are, in any case, no other examples in the book to compare them with, and if they were intended to imply something, whether textual or emotional, the meaning was lost very quickly. Fulke Greville, editing his friend's novel, presumably understood them, since he retained them in his edition of 1593. In the Countess of Pembroke's 1598 folio edition, however, wonderful,& almoſt matchleſſe excellécy in matters of armes. *Pyrocles* vſed diuers faynings,to bring *Anaxius* on, into ſome inconuenience. But *Anaxius* keeping a ſound maner of fighting,neuer offered,but ſeeing faire cauſe, & then followed it with wel-gouerned violence. Thus ſpent they a great time,ſtriuing to doo , and with ſtriuing to doo , wearying themſelues,more then with the very doing. *Anaxius* finding *Zelmane* ſo neere vnto him , that with little motion he might reach her , knitting all his ſtrength together , at that time mainly foyned at her face. But *Zelmane* ſtrongly putting it by with her right hande ſword, comming in with her left foote, and hand woulde haue giuen him a ſharpe viſitation to his right ſide , but that he was faine to leape away. Whereat aſhamed, (as hauing neuer done ſo much before in his life)

Figure 4. Sir Philip Sidney, *The Countesse of Pembrokes Arcadia* (1590), fol. 360ᵛ, the concluding page of text.

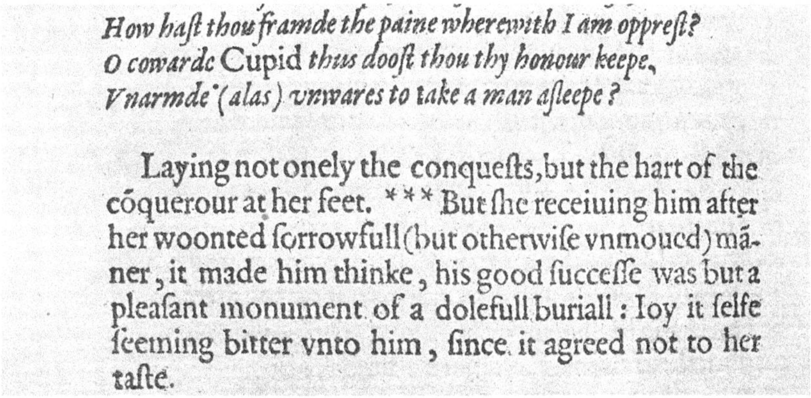

How haſt thou framde the paine wherewith I am oppreſt?
O cowarde Cupid *thus dooſt thou thy honour keepe,*
Vnarmde˚(alas) vnwares to take a man aſleepe?

Laying not onely the conqueſts,but the hart of the
coquerour at her feet. *** But ſhe receiuing him after
her woonted ſorrowfull(but otherwiſe vnmoued)må-
ner, it made him thinke, his good ſucceſſe was but a
pleaſant monument of a dolefull buriall : Ioy it ſelfe
ſeeming bitter vnto him , ſince it agreed not to her
taſte.

Figure 5. Sir Philip Sidney, *The Countesse of Pembrokes Arcadia* (1590), fol. 275ᵛ.

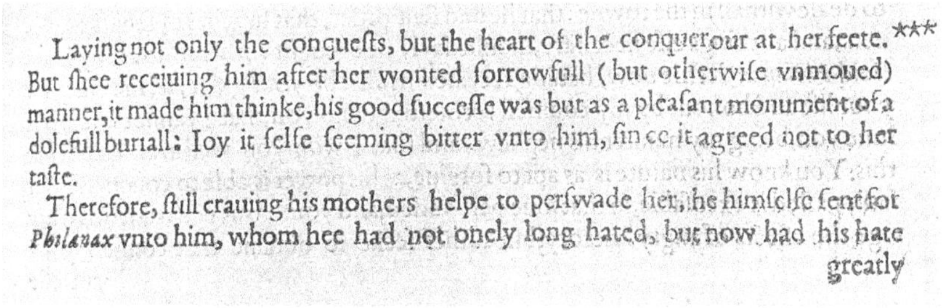

Laying not only the conqueſts, but the heart of the conquerour at her feete. ***
But ſhee receiuing him after her wonted ſorrowfull (but otherwiſe vnmoued)
manner, it made him thinke,his good ſucceſſe was but as a pleaſant monument of a
dolefull buriall: Ioy it ſelfe ſeeming bitter vnto him, ſince it agreed not to her
taſte.
    Therefore, ſtill crauing his mothers helpe to perſwade her, he himſelfe ſent for
Philanax vnto him, whom hee had not onely long hated, but now had his hate
                                                                        greatly

Figure 6. Sir Philip Sidney, *The Countesse of Pembrokes Arcadia* (1605), 263.

they have moved, quite pointlessly, into the margin, where they remained in
the folio of 1605 (Figure 6), and they finally disappeared in editions after 1613.

The empty parentheses of Sonnet 126, then, are not following any typographic tradition. And whatever they meant to the compositor, and however
temporary they were intended to be, they remained in the book as a feature of
the text. What did they signify to a reader in 1609? And what do they signify
now? Editors have been divided about whether to remove them. The poem
is not included in John Benson's 1640 version, but in Bernard Lintot's 1709
reprint of the original edition the parentheses have taken on a life of their
own: the twelve lines of the poem occupy the lower portion of volume 2, page
69, and the poem appears to end there. The catchword is this: ( ). Figure 7
shows the beginning of page 70.

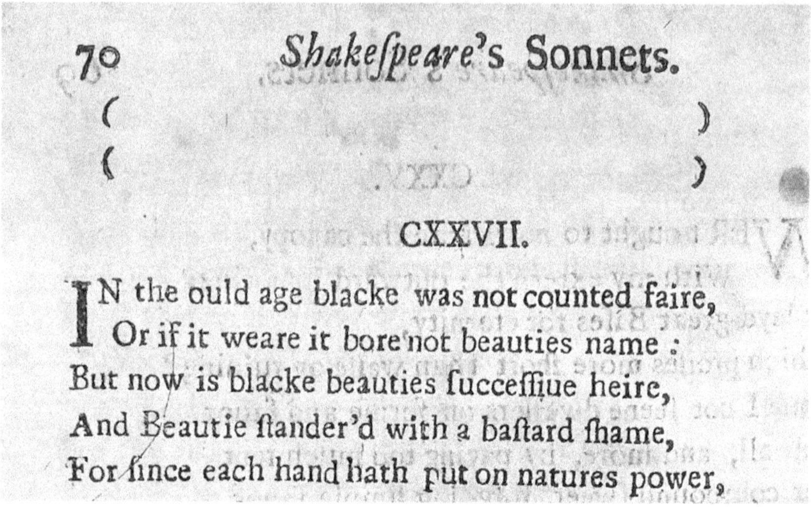

70   *Shakespeare's* Sonnets.

( )

( )

CXXVII.

IN the ould age blacke was not counted faire,
Or if it weare it bore not beauties name ;
But now is blacke beauties fucceffiue heire,
And Beautie flander'd with a baftard fhame,
For fince each hand hath put on natures power,

Figure 7. The concluding brackets of Sonnet 126 in 1709. *A Collection of Poems, in Two Volumes; Being all the Miscellanies of Mr. William Shakespeare* . . . (1709), vol. 2, 70.

It should be emphasized that page 70 is the *verso* of page 69; the parentheses therefore do not face the rest of the poem and are not obviously part of it. It is difficult to imagine what any reader was expected to make of this, but clearly the typographer's instructions were to stick firmly to his copy text.[8] Malone's 1780 edition, the first critical edition based on the 1609 text, omits the parentheses, and does not even mention their existence. Most modern editions conclude the poem with its final couplet. Stephen Booth's Yale edition is characteristically equivocal, including the parentheses in his facsimile but omitting them in the modernized version on the facing page—they are both there and not there. His note explains that the printer included them "apparently to indicate that he thought there was something missing"; Booth clearly thinks there is nothing missing. But Colin Burrow, in the best modern edition, is quite firm—even lyrically so—in rejecting this argument: "Many editors omit the brackets as compositorial. As a part of the typographical effect of Q they should certainly be retained: they highlight the frustrated expectations created by the poem's form. The curves of the lunulae (or brackets) may graphically evoke both a crescent moon and the curve of Time's sickle . . . The effect is deliberately of abrupt termination, as in Hotspur's dying lines, 'No, Percy, thou art dust/ And food for———'"[9]

Well perhaps, but Hotspur's dying lines end with a very long dash, not with a set of empty parentheses. John Kerrigan's brilliant Penguin edition makes a similar argument, but, on the contrary, removes the parentheses, although declaring them "conceivably authorial, but more likely added by a scribe or someone connected with the script's publishing or printing" and continues, "these brackets are excluded . . . not without regret, as accidentals. What they usefully point up in Q is a sense of poetic shortfall, as though the recoiling, inconclusive quality of earlier sonnet couplets . . . had been concentrated in a single poem, consisting entirely of such rhymed endings, which 'rounded off' the sub-sequence . . . without solving by aesthetic means the problems it addressed."[10]

Wow: if accidentals can do all that, should they really be removed?

Sonnet 126 remains an anomaly; with or without the parentheses, many aspects of the poem beg for an explanation. It is usually described (or perhaps defended) as a conclusion to the poems to the beloved young man, and it is certainly true that whoever put the collection together must have sensed that some transition was necessary from the abject homoeroticism of Sonnet 125, "No, let me be obsequious in thy heart,/And take thou my oblation, poor but free," to the cynical womanizing of Sonnet 127, "In the old age black was not counted fair." The change of tone represented by Sonnet 126 is indeed radical: this is not the lovely boy for whom the poet "bore the canopy"; this youth is not being urged to marry, or to love the poet, or even to allow the poet to love him. This boy is Nature's minion, and Nature is as fickle as the young man has been. The poet offers no immortalizing verse, only the most detached of warnings, not even to make use of time, but only to fear it—in the drama of the sequence, the admonition is a little smug, even perhaps a little vengeful: desirable as you are, you're just like the rest of us. Couplets at this point in the sequence have served to interrupt or reverse or turn off one hundred and twenty-five sonnets. Sonnet 126 seems to ask, will six more couplets do it? And the parentheses say, will just one more, will seven?

Hardly. The transition merely moves the poet from desiring an irresistible, epicene, faithless, deceitful, unresponsive man to desiring an irresistible, dark,

faithless, lascivious, adulterous woman. It seems clear that though the sonnets were written at different periods over many years, their arrangement into
individual groups must have been Shakespeare's; but their organization into a
published volume is a different matter. If the placement of Sonnet 126 makes
sense, what about Sonnet 145, the epigram on Anne Hathaway's name, another
anomaly, the only tetrameter sonnet, bizarrely placed between "Two loves have
I of comfort and despair" (neither one, clearly, Shakespeare's wife) and "Poor
soul, the center of my sinful earth," which has nothing to do with women or
love at all? Sonnet 145 alone, of all the poems in the sequence, certifies the poet
as Shakespeare—awkwardly, for critics who want to argue that the speaker of
the sonnets is not to be construed as the author, that the love for the young
man no more implies that Shakespeare was gay than *Macbeth* implies that he
was a murderer. But given the relentless anonymity of the young man, the dark
lady, the rival poet, why would a compiler want to identify Shakespeare at this
point, especially through a punning sonnet about his wife? Sonnet 135, beginning "Whoever hath her wish, thou hast thy Will,/And Will to boot, and Will
in over-plus," merely teases us with autobiography—the author is named Will,
but so is the speaker, and the friend, and the lady's husband: much wit but
not much information there. What about the final two sonnets, lighthearted
epigrams modelled on the Greek Anthology? They seem, to say the least, out
of place: did Shakespeare really have anything to do with concluding his emotionally fraught sequence with them? How do you end this cycle of desire,
frustration, and abjection?

   And what of the conclusion of the volume itself? *Shake-speare's Sonnets*
ends with the long lament *A Lovers Complaint*. Its presence in the volume
remains a puzzle; but given the "lovely boy" couplets, the Anne Hathaway
tetrameters, and the Palatine epigrams, perhaps it is less of a puzzle than it
has been made to be. The publisher Thomas Thorpe obviously considered it
an appropriate way of concluding the book, but whether Shakespeare did, or
whether it was part of the same manuscript, or whether Shakespeare wrote it
at all, are impossible questions to answer with any certainty. Thorpe believed
that he had written it, explicitly including Shakespeare's name after the title—
there is no reason to suspect any misrepresentation in this. But in cases where

the author is not involved in a book's publication, the ascription of even a perfectly reputable publisher in the period has only limited value.

To conclude a volume of sonnets with a long poem was not unusual: Spenser's *Amoretti* concludes with the *Epithalamion*, Daniel's *Delia* with *The Complaint of Rosamond*. As for the question of authorship, critics remained dubious about the matter until the 1960s. The poem is in the same stanza form as *Lucrece* but includes a number of archaisms uncharacteristic of Shakespeare and forty-nine words or forms found nowhere else in his works. This vocabulary evidence against Shakespeare's authorship has been countered by the argument that plays that are unquestionably Shakespeare's often employ new vocabulary, including new verbs made from nouns and newly invented compound adjectives, and that therefore the unusual and unique usages could indicate, on the contrary, that the poem is in fact by Shakespeare. This argument may, of course, merely constitute evidence of how manipulable stylometric analysis can be. In the past two decades, several impressive critical readings of the poem have insisted that it is both authentically Shakespearean and has an integral place among the sonnets.[11] Colin Burrow, in the most authoritative recent essay on Shakespeare's poems, declares discussion about the poem's attribution "definitively ended."[12] But consensus remains elusive: Brian Vickers, shortly after the declaration of the definitive end of discussion, ascribed the poem to John Davies of Hereford.[13]

Of course, the poem may well have sounded like Shakespeare to Thorpe: the sound of Shakespeare is not a constant. Robert Allott's anthology *England's Parnassus* (1600) ascribes John of Gaunt's dying speech from *Richard II* to Michael Drayton and several passages by William Warner to Shakespeare. Shakespeare does not sound to us like Drayton or Warner, but in 1600, at least to one reader, he did. All we can say with absolute confidence is that to read the sonnets as the readers of Thorpe's quarto did—which is to say, as Shakespeare's contemporaries did—we must take *A Lovers Complaint* into account.

And in fact, *A Lovers Complaint* does provide a conclusion of a sort, the same sort of conclusion that Sonnet 126, with its empty parentheses, provides to the drama of the love poems to the young man: it represents a reversal, perhaps even a kind of revenge. The lover here has turned the tables. The speaker is a young woman abandoned by her beloved, desolate, yet at the end quite clear about the fact that she will never be free of him, that another glance from him would win her back:

> O, that infected moisture of his eye,
> O, that false fire which in his cheek so glowed. . .
> Would yet again betray the fore-betrayed,
> And new pervert a reconcilèd maid. (lines 323–329)

What this conclusion says is that implicit in the sequence is an alternative scenario, already suggested in the poems about the intruding mistress and the rival poet, and fully articulated in the sonnets to the deceitful dark lady, in which the protagonist's abjection turns resentful, sarcastic, cynical, and witty. These look ahead to a poetry in which lyric concessiveness is reconceived as dramatic vindictiveness and in which the wit of the lyric sequence is refigured into a drama where the poet, the witty deviser of conceits, schemes, and devices, really is in control. This plot begins where the sonnets end, with the failure of the love, and it shows the master of language and argument getting his own back, the dramatic poet avenging himself on the lyric subject. In *A Lovers Complaint* the scenario is still seen from the viewpoint of the victim. As I discuss in more detail in the essay "Lascivious Grace," the reversal will be fully articulated by the poet of *Othello*, with its villain a witty deviser of schemes and conceits who says, if I can't make you love me I can make you hate me; if I can't give you life, I can take it away. Iago's drama concludes with a dramatic version of an empty parenthesis: "Demand me nothing. What you know you know./From this time forth I never will speak word."

—(2013)

4

Lascivious Grace

Seductive Evil in Shakespeare and Jonson

I begin with the conclusion of Shakespeare's Sonnet 40, the acknowledgment of betrayal and incorrigible faithlessness in the beloved young man, which is at the same time an acknowledgment of his irresistible attractiveness:

> Lascivious grace, in whom all ill well shows,
> Kill me with spites yet we must not be foes.

"In whom all ill well shows": there is nothing in the sonnets to equal or counteract the seductive power of "lascivious grace," no sustaining counter-principle of virtue and fidelity. In Sonnet 144, about the poet's "two loves . . . of comfort and despair," even the poet's "good angel" is inevitably "fired out" by his bad one; indeed, the implication is that the two angels have been lovers. Equivocation and ambivalence form a litany throughout the sonnets, but the bad always wins. The poet of the sonnets is megalomaniacal about the power of his verse, but given all the boasting about the defeat of time and the conferral of immortality, it is the abjectness of this poet that is striking, the repeated insistence that the beloved, even as he betrays the poet with a mistress or prefers a rival poet, is too good for him, that the poet-lover deserves the neglect he suffers, and that the love, however compelling, however much the source of a poetry more lasting than monuments, is nothing but a flattering dream.

Nevertheless, as I have suggested in "No Sense of an Ending," implicit in Shakespeare's sequence is an alternative scenario, in which the protagonist's abjection turns resentful, sarcastic, cynical, and very witty. This scenario is already suggested in the poems about the intruding mistress and the rival poet and is fully articulated in the sonnets to the deceitful dark lady. The original *Shake-speares Sonnets*, the volume in which the poems first appeared in 1609, in fact concludes in this way, with the long Spenserian lament *A Lovers Complaint*. This may or may not be by Shakespeare, but the publisher believed it was Shakespeare's, and more important, believed that it was an appropriate conclusion to the volume. I have discussed the poem in "No Sense of an Ending": *A Lovers Complaint* is spoken by a forsaken woman, seduced and abandoned by an eloquent charmer—the betrayed poet-lover has finally turned the tables, not only on his mistress, but also on all women, on all lovers. This plot begins where the sonnets end, with betrayal and frustration. And as Shakespeare pursues and develops the theme in his drama, it shows the master of language and argument getting his own back, the dramatic poet avenging himself on the lyric subject. This poet says, if I can't make you love me I can make you hate me; if I can't give you, life I can take it away. Dramatically, the sonnets culminate not in triumphant creativity but in relentless malice and vindictiveness —the true poet of the sonnets is not Prospero but Iago. The repeated lyric claim that "my friend and I are one" achieves a dangerous dramatic reality as Iago declares to Othello that "I am your own forever" and asserts that "In following him I follow but myself."

I developed this argument in an essay called "Othello and the End of Comedy," and my next section is based on that essay.[1] Stephen Greenblatt long ago suggested, in *Renaissance Self-Fashioning*, that Iago, as the amoral manipulator and endlessly fertile improviser of plots, was a figure for Shakespeare, but I am suggesting something much more psychologically and emotionally specific. In the most straightforward view of the plot, Iago is the agent of all the play's destructiveness and bad faith, the source of all the tragic energy—in short, the villain. A little less straightforwardly, he is certainly still the villain, but perhaps nevertheless not the agent and source at all. He is merely the catalyst, externalizing and articulating the destructive chaos that lies just beneath Othello's love and rationality, the chaos that he himself says is kept in check only by his love for Desdemona—rather like the witches in *Macbeth*, or, indeed, Lady Macbeth herself, who, however evil, are not the culprits. A lot depends on how far we want to regard Iago as a classic machiavel on the one hand, or as an extension of Othello on the other. The latter might seem to be a post-Renaissance conception, but in fact the play itself questions the simple view of Iago's malign responsibility for Othello's behavior when Emilia remarks that jealous souls "are not ever jealous for the cause,/But jealous for they are jealous." Othello's jealousy is not, then, simply the creation of Iago's scheming. There is a good deal of self-interest in this piece of wisdom, of course, since Emilia herself has provided the trigger of Othello's jealousy, the handkerchief, and is covering for both herself and her husband long after she understands quite clearly the mischief she has caused; but the observation is, nevertheless, also self-evidently true, and it is a truth around which Iago designs his scheme.

Villain and victim, in fact, have much more in common and understand each other much better than husband and wife: it is clear that Iago's cynical view of women as lustful, untrustworthy, and characteristically unfaithful is, when the chips are down, Othello's view also, and therefore Othello instinctively believes in Iago's honesty, not in his wife's—this is true from the first moment Desdemona's fidelity is questioned; all Iago has to say is "I think Cassio's an honest man." One could argue, indeed, that the source of the tragedy is precisely in that gender bonding, or its neglect—in the fact that Othello's primary loyalty is to his friend, not his wife; in the fact that Emilia chooses to betray her mistress, not her husband. But it is also possible to imagine this play without Iago: certainly all those elements of jealousy, self dramatization, rage, and barely controlled chaos that Iago elicits are aspects of Othello's character clearly articulated from the outset.

In staging the play, to make Iago a sort of allegorical extension of Othello would, of course, make for a much more complex Othello than we are used to, one that would continually raise the question of how far the play's claim that the tragedy is all Iago's fault, which is essentially a claim that jealousy is explicable and reasonable—that men get jealous because villains steal handkerchiefs and tell lies—is borne out by the action. There are two ways of reading "In following him I follow but myself": as Iago's assertion of total self-interest in his relation to Othello, or alternatively, as an acknowledgment that, in a much deeper sense, they are inseparable. The bond can be construed as a love relationship, with Iago's resentment that of a scorned lover, rejected in favor of Cassio on the one hand and Desdemona on the other, a rejection all the more painful because it has been so casual. The jealousy, then, in the first instance would be Iago's. He presents himself again as a scorned lover when he accuses both Cassio and Othello of sleeping with his wife Emilia. This is basically the situation dramatized in the *Sonnets*, and if we take that sequence to be in any sense autobiographical, Shakespeare is depicting himself in Iago—not only as Greenblatt's "amoral manipulator and endlessly fertile improvisor of plots," but as the sonnets' jealous lover as well:

> So shall I live, believing thou art true
> Like a deceived husband. . . .

—but a cuckold who finally catches on

If we are thinking of Shakespeare's dramaturgy in terms of autobiography, here is another proposition: we know that Richard Burbage played Othello, but in Shakespeare's company who played the much larger role of Iago? Iago is one of the longest roles in Shakespeare—1,020 lines, almost 250 lines longer than Othello. Only Hamlet, the longest role by far, and Richard III are longer; these three are the only roles that are over a thousand lines (though Henry V almost makes it, at 999). For comparison, the whole of *The Comedy of Errors* is only 1,750 lines long, and *Macbeth* just over 2,000. Iago is a third of his play. Could it be a part that Shakespeare the actor wrote for himself?

Probably the answer is no; the one Shakespearian role we think we know Shakespeare played was Adam in *As You Like It*, and a much more apocryphal tradition has him as the Ghost in *Hamlet*. These stories at least suggest that the roles he took in his own plays were small ones; and John Lowin, who we know played the villainous Bosola in *The Duchess of Malfi* and the ill-tempered Morose in *Epicoene*, had joined the company in 1603 and would therefore have been available. Nevertheless the *Sonnets* provide an inescapable gloss on all the painful ramifications of the assumption that "My friend and I are one." The identity, the interchangeability, of Othello and Iago has been a significant part of stage history for centuries, perhaps always. If the original Iago was not Shakespeare, and even if it was Lowin, did Burbage nevertheless, like Garrick, Edmund Kean, Kemble, Macready, Fechter, Irving, Edwin Booth, Olivier, and even, unlikely as it sounds, Gielgud, play both roles, and were the roles, from the beginning, interchangeable; did the great actor always want to be both? Virtuoso performers, starting with Edmund Kean and Charles Mayne Young, and including Macready and Samuel Phelps, Edwin Booth and Henry Irving, and Richard Burton and John Neville, have even alternated the roles, sometimes from night to night, playing out, in the most literal way, "Were I the Moor, I would not be Iago." In fact, Kean, as Iago, refused to switch after he saw the first night of Young's Othello, convinced he could never equal it—Iago's envy was in this case the very essence of performance itself.

Throughout the eighteenth and much of the nineteenth centuries, the machiavellian Iago, innately evil and an obvious extension of Richard III, often outfitted, in the absence of a hunchback, with diabolically bushy eyebrows and black wig, was standard; but from the time of Fechter and Irving, Iago has tended to be the really complex character in the play. A good deal of the cumulative effect of the drama depends on how the actor decides to play him. Most productions have made him complex but unattractive, saturnine, insinuating, crude, graceless—most of all, not a gentleman. In such performances, the real energy of the role goes into the villainy—it is a melodramatic energy, undeniably effective, but it simplifies the play, makes him a villain like Richard III, where his villainy is in every sense his defining characteristic. In the case of Richard III, his success is represented first as a political phenomenon, where he is supported by people who are either naively trusting or think he is horrible but will do them some good, and second—notoriously, in the wooing of Lady Anne—as a kind of mesmeric magic, because he is so obviously villainous. The problem with treating Iago this way is that such a reading does not make enough distinction between the public and the private Iago—Richard is always a villain, but until the final scene, we know much more about Iago than any of the characters do, and there has to be some reason established dramatically for why everyone finds him so implicitly trustworthy. Dramatically, making him unattractive and graceless accounts for his hostility and resentment but does nothing to explain his extraordinary persuasiveness.

As I stage the play in my own mind, he is attractive and very charming. The only performance I have ever seen that was anything like this was Kenneth Branagh's, in the film with Laurence Fishburn as Othello. There were lots of problems with this film—Fishburn looked wonderful but didn't do much with the verse; Irene Jacob's English was so heavily accented that she might have been in some other play—but the Iago was a revelation: easygoing, affable, good looking, affectionate, an instant best friend, somebody you wanted to confide in and have around. In this performance, the melodrama is saved for the soliloquies, so that Iago is completely different in public and in private. Branagh gives the film the sense of a stage performance by talking directly to the camera (rather than "thinking" his soliloquies); he plays with the audience, taking them into his confidence, making them his accomplices, charming them, flirting with them, just as he does not so much persuade Roderigo and Cassio but woos them.

I would even take this a step farther and take the analogy of the *Sonnets* into account, making Iago an attractive gay man seriously in love with Othello, and Othello a narcissist, not at all averse to being adored and fully trusting Iago because he trusts his own attractiveness; knowing, moreover, that he does not have to promote Iago, because he is perfectly aware of his sexual power over his subordinate. (My use of the shorthand term "gay" is anachronistic only in the sense that the term is modern; there have always been men who fell in love with other men.) The sexual dynamic here would be a two-way affair, and when, in this production of mine, Othello elicits from Iago the words of the marriage vow, "I am your own forever," he is quite conscious of what he is doing. After all, throughout the play Othello is under the impression that he is using Iago, not the other way around—"Prove my love a whore"; "Within these three days let me hear thee say/That Cassio's not alive." The fantasy of replacing Desdemona with Iago as his wife is in my production parallel to Iago's fantasy of lying awake in bed with Cassio asleep (or pretending to be) and sexually excited, taking Iago for Desdemona (or pretending to). Is Othello's fury at this solely at the idea of Cassio imagining he is in bed with Desdemona? Is the idea of Cassio actually making love to Iago no part of it? Quite possibly the answer is no; nevertheless, one may resist the sexual implications, but the homoeroticism is undeniable: it is obvious that the crucial relationships in both these episodes are between the men. As in the *Sonnets*, who knows how much is implied by "My friend and I are one" and "I am your own forever"?

Two friends to whom I have proposed this haven't liked it; both objected that making Iago gay explains too much, that the malignity ought to be left motiveless. I am surprised that love is assumed to constitute more of an explanation than hatred; but in any case, Iago does explain at some length why he hates Othello—the problem is really that he offers too many motives, not too few. Cassio has a daily beauty in his life that makes Iago's ugly, Othello has preferred Cassio to him, Othello and Cassio have been to bed with his wife—all the explanations boil down to envy and jealousy; and as Romeo (that is, Shakespeare) says, "Here's much to do with hate, but more with love." Coleridge's point in characterizing Iago as "motiveless malignity" was surely that the explanations don't really explain anything, don't produce a rational motive, but instead produce only jealousy, or hatred (or love), not that they aren't there. Romeo cites not only the inseparability of love and hate, but the motivelessness of both as well: "Why then, O brawling love, O loving hate,/O anything of nothing first create!" (I.174–176).

In "Othello and the End of Comedy" I cited some productions that have in fact accounted for Iago's behavior by suggesting that he was gay. Tyrone Guthrie in 1938 had Laurence Olivier as a homosexual Iago furtively longing for Ralph Richardson's Othello, though no critics caught on to the fact that Iago was supposed to be gay, and Guthrie shortly abandoned the interpretation. Nevertheless, Olivier declared the production a disaster (the gay Iago was obviously not the culprit). In Terry Hands's 1985 RSC production with Ben Kingsley as Othello and David Suchet as Iago, Iago was widely perceived as gay, and the performance was well received, not least because by 1985 it was permissible to acknowledge publicly that someone was gay. Hands apparently did not intend Iago to be gay and was surprised at the reviews. David Suchet, however, in a thoughtful interview about the performance in one of the *Players of Shakespeare* volumes, says that he considered the possibility at some length.[2] He decided that the account of the night spent with Cassio is a lie, though a significant one. He thought it quite conceivable that Iago and Cassio may in fact have been lovers and that Othello may well be jealous of the idea that they have been to bed together—Suchet was, in short, on to my idea long before it

occurred to me, and I am interested to see that an intelligent and thoughtful
actor seriously considered it as a way of making the character work psychologically. By the end of the twentieth century, we had an openly gay Mercutio
who goes partying in drag in Baz Luhrman's 1996 *Romeo and Juliet*. My students liked this, and when I asked what they liked about it one young woman
explained that "cool gay guys are really neat." I want my Iago to be a cool gay
guy, a Iago who is all the more dangerous because both Othello and more than
half the audience find him attractive. The play's vice then becomes its prime
dramatic virtue—as Sonnet 119 sums it up,

> O benefit of ill! Now I find true
> That better is by evil still made better;
> And ruined love, when it is built anew,
> Grows fairer than at first, more strong, far greater.
> So I return rebuked to my content,
> And gain by ills thrice more than I have spent.

Shakespeare's alter-ego, the playwright who takes this principle to heart
and makes vice into the central dramatic virtue, is surely Ben Jonson, for
whom the Iago figure, the schemer, the clever scoundrel, is the great comic
principle. Arguably this notion is central to the history of theater itself—think
of the ubiquitous machinations that propel the comedy of Aristophanes,
refined and personified into the scheming, scamming slave-heroes of Roman
comedy. A millennium later one may have gone to morality plays for the good
of one's soul, to see virtue triumphant and evil vanquished, but most of the
energy, and therefore the pleasure, of those plays in performance was precisely
in the vice figures—iniquity was where the fun was. That same vicious energy
remained the central comic principle in the tragedy of *Doctor Faustus*, and
those scenes of diabolical fun, in which the interaction of humanity with the
infernal powers produces not the fear of damnation but the pleasures of farce,
were the scenes that were continually augmented over the several centuries
of the play's life on the stage. Even *Macbeth*, Shakespeare's most powerful
dramatization of incarnate evil, was within a decade of its composition being
expanded with interpolated scenes of dances and songs for the witches—by

the 1660s Pepys could declare it "a most excellent play in all respects, but especially in divertisement," though he acknowledged that that was "a strange perfection in a tragedy."[3] Most tragedies weren't this much fun, and the divertisement was provided by the incarnations of evil.

Jonson was certainly a moralist, and his ethical pronouncements are ubiquitous throughout his poetry. But if we consider his two masterpieces *Volpone* and *The Alchemist*, the moral claims appear ambiguous at best. The schemers are, of course, not diabolical machiavels but small time crooks, but they epitomize a vision of society as thoroughly corrupt, and if we see that as something less than evil we only reveal our own complicity in it. Jonson makes the implication explicit in *The Devil Is an Ass*, his morality play of 1616, which follows *Bartholomew Fair* and sums up a decade of social indictment. In it a devil is sent to earth to do the Devil's work and is thoroughly conned and gulled by his mortal prey: in the practice of villainy, the diabolical is no match for the human—everyone is guilty. That this is a subject for comedy indicates how naturalized the assumption was for Jonson's age.

There is a seriously divided aesthetic in Jonson. Consider the poetry of *The Alchemist*. On the one hand, Jonson's fondness for epigram is on display—he declared his epigrams "the ripest of my studies,"[4] and Martial was his favorite poet. Certainly when Subtle, Face, and Doll are fighting there are lots of real zingers; but on the other hand, think of the compulsive aggregation of the big extended speeches such as Sir Epicure Mammon's fantasies of fulfilled desire, which work like operatic arias. In the same way, in his greatest poems, Jonson writes extended eulogies to the lavish hospitality of the Sidneys at Penshurst and to Sir Robert Wroth or celebrates the sumptuous food promised in the poem *Inviting a Friend to Supper*. Mammon's arias go on and on, but he isn't a bore, he's a crazy genius—those are high points in the play. Sometimes Jonson makes himself out to be an ethical stoic, idealizing withdrawal from the world, but much more often he is the most materialistic poet in English: he loves the world; especially he loves things—Mammon or Volpone speak with the voice of early modern capitalism. They worship wealth. Volpone opens with a hymn to money: "Good morning to the day, and next, my gold./Open the shrine, that I may see my saint." What such characters want is the best of everything, which means not platonic ideals, but the rarest and richest consumer goods that money can buy. The voice of the epicure is also the voice of the collector and connoisseur; these plays are all about taste, and whatever your ideals are, you can't fulfill them without a great deal of money. Even Jonson's poetry celebrating the virtues of his patrons is about money—the boundless hospitality of the Sidney family or the taste and generosity of the Countess of Bedford depend on a very large income.

Where is the moral center of any of these plays? Lovewit, the offstage master of *The Alchemist*, sounds like a name for the hero of a play about the intellect, love-wit, but he is merely the beneficiary of the clever scoundrel he employs, who buys off his potential indignation with a rich widow to marry. The wit he loves is the ingenuity of his servant, the con man Face; and though the relentlessly skeptical Pertinax Surly keeps saying he won't be gulled, in fact nobody in the play sees through the deceptions. Is there a moral center in this play? All the energy is clearly in the material goods on the one hand and the ingenuity of the plotting on the other; Subtle, Face, and Doll are essentially playwrights, the endlessly creative inventors of plots, just like Jonson. The ethical figures are there to be either indulgent, like Lovewit, or gulled and abused, like Ananias. In the same way, the good people in *Volpone*, Celia and Bonario, don't win because they're good, they win because the fox outfoxes himself; the con game in *The Alchemist* ends because the schemes fall apart from their own complexity. The endings, moreover, are profoundly ambiguous: Mosca loses in the end, but he could just as easily end up a millionaire; one thing goes wrong. Face wins in the end, but he could just as easily end up in jail; one thing goes right. If Jonson had written a version of *Othello* it would be all about Iago, but one wonders how the play would have ended. It is not surprising that one of Jonson's earliest plays, which he chose not to preserve, was *Richard Crookback*, a tragedy about Richard III. The villainous hero was where he started—the subject was a natural one for him.

What is the moral to Jonson's comedies of evil? It is certainly not "be virtuous." If you're a crook, be smart, but don't overdo it. If you're greedy, don't be a megalomaniac. Be skeptical; but you'll be cheated anyway. Above all, choose your servants very carefully, but don't trust them too far. Is Jonson a cynic? Hardly: he takes too much pleasure in his inventions.

—(2016)

5

The Poetics of Incomprehensibility

Stage procedures and their importance, as embedded in the texts that remain to us, have yet to be looked at outside of the rubric of the assumptions about method that we have inherited from the Enlightenment.

—Marion Trousdale

I

I begin with two notoriously obscure passages in *The Winter's Tale*—by no means the most obscure, at least for modern readers. Both are from Hermione's trial scene. The first has Hermione, in the course of her objections to the proceedings, say to Leontes,

> I appeale
> To your owne Conscience (Sir) before *Polixenes*
> Came to your Court, how I was in your grace,
> How merited to be so: Since he came,
> With what encounter so uncurrant, I
> Have strayn'd t'appeare thus (3.2.44–49)[1]

For the past hundred and fifty years or so, the last two lines have been taken to mean "with what behavior so unacceptable I have transgressed that I should appear thus [i.e., on trial]." This interpretation represents the consensus of three mid-Victorian editors, Halliwell, Staunton, and White, and it has become, for us, simply the meaning of the passage.

But to gloss the passage in this way is, at the very least, to conceal more than a century of debate and bafflement. The lines were, in fact, considered incomprehensible by most eighteenth-century editors, including Samuel Johnson, who wrote of them, "These lines I do not understand; with the license of all editors, what I cannot understand I suppose unintelligible, and therefore propose that they may be altered."[2] Johnson's testimony in this matter is especially *à propos* given his characteristic genius for finding a plain prose sense in the most elaborately conceited Shakespearean verse. In default of an interpretation, he produced a felicitous, if unconvincingly rationalized, emendation: "With what encounter so uncurrant *have I/Been stain'd* to appear thus?" Even this, though it certainly makes a kind of sense, depends on its emendation to render the crucially ambiguous words *encounter* and *uncurrent* comprehensible. A detailed consideration of the history of similar attempts at elucidation would show no more then do the relevant *OED* entries for *encounter, uncurrent,* and *strain*: that the modern interpretation represents an arbitrary selection of meanings from a list of diverse and often contradictory possibilities and does not so much resolve the linguistic problem as enable us to ignore it.

Consider another example. Hermione, later in the scene recalling her recent childbirth confinement, objects that she has been

                                   hurried

Here, to this place, I'th'open ayre, before
I have got strength of limit. (3.2.103–105)

In this case the Victorian editors were as divided as their predecessors. Theobald thought "strength of limit" must mean "strength enough for coming abroad, going never so little a way." Heath in 1765 found a rather garrulous sense in the passage: "before I have recovered that degree of strength which women in my circumstances usually acquire by a longer confinement to their chamber." Halliwell in the next century produced a different and more economical paraphrase, "that is, before even I have regained a limited degree of strength," and explained that "strength of limit" is "*limited strength.*" White, in 1858, endorsed a version of Heath's interpretation of a century earlier: "before I have regained strength by limit, restraint, confinement after childbirth." H. H. Furness, reviewing the controversy in 1898, rendered a characteristically judicious opinion: "If it could be proved that 'limit' had a special meaning, corresponding to what is now called, with special meaning, *confinement*, the interpretations referring to child-birth would be unquestionable, but, without this proof, I think Halliwell's paraphrase the best." Johnson, the greatest of explicators, had once again confessed himself baffled and once again took refuge in an emendation: "I know not well how 'strength of limit' can mean strength *to pass the limits* of the child-bed chamber; which yet it must mean in this place, unless we read in a more easy phrase, 'strength of *limb.*'" It was only in the twentieth century that a consensus was reached. Dover Wilson and Quiller-Couch in the Cambridge New Shakespeare *Winter's Tale*, followed by virtually all subsequent editors, returned to Heath's explanation of 1765, glossing the crucial words in this way: "the strength which returns to a woman when she has rested the prescribed period after child-birth."[3] Their confident note gives no hint of two centuries of uncertainty, debate, and disagreement.

But convenient as the modern interpretation is, the *OED* in fact offers little support for it. The entry for *limit* cites only two examples of the word meaning a prescribed time, Hermione's passage and one from *Measure for Measure*, "between the time of the contract and limit of the solemnity." It is not, however, clear to me that this is in fact the same usage: *limit* in the *Measure for Measure* passage means not a period of time but a *terminus ad quem*, the date fixed for Mariana's marriage to Angelo. J. H. P. Pafford added a more persuasive example from *Richard III*: "the limit of your life is out."[4] This example, however, is much less elliptical than Hermione's, and the expression in relation to childbed is unparalleled. By 1663 the phrase in *The Winter's Tale* was already being emended; in F3 and F4 as well as in editions by Rowe, Pope, and Hanmer, Hermione's "limit" became "limbs." And though the emendation was not generally accepted after this time, the interpretive problem remained, and, as we have seen, Johnson found the emendation attractive enough to return to it.

I have focused on these two cases because they are relatively simple ones. Though the particular expressions are obscure, Hermione's general drift is clear enough for us to see what we have to get her words to mean. What is concealed in the process of interpretation—to which Johnson's methods constitute a striking exception—is the effort of will, or even willfulness, involved. This method of elucidation assumes that behind the obscurity and confusion of the text is a clear meaning and that the obscurity, moreover, is not part of the meaning.

II

But what are the implications for drama of a text that works in this way? Hermione's speeches are, as I have said, simple cases, discrete moments that at least appear to leave the larger sense of the passage intact. Leontes's invective in Act I gives us no such confidence:

> Can thy Dam, may't be
> Affection? thy Intention stabs the Center.
> Thou do'st make possible things not so held,
> Communicat'st with Dreames (how can this be?)
> With what's unreall: thou coactive art,
> And fellow'st nothing. Then 'tis very credent,
> Thou may'st co-joyne with something, and thou do'st,
> (And that beyond Commission) and I find it (1.2.138–145)

Find *what*? From Rowe onward the passage has defied any consensus. Indeed, it is one of the rare places where Rowe, normally the most tolerant of editors, felt moved to radical revision: "Can thy dam? may't be—/Imagination! thou dost stab to the center." This can hardly be called emendation. And though no subsequent editor was persuaded, most editions since Rowe's time have adopted his equally radical repunctuation, whereby "may't be" stands alone, and "Affection," no longer a predicate nominative in the simple question "may't be Affection?" is now the vocative subject of a new sentence, "Affection, thy intention stabs the center!"

My purpose is not to propose a new reading or to announce the matter resolved (though I cannot help remarking that I find some of the problems greatly simplified if we reject the ubiquitous and quite unnecessary repunctuation). What interests me is how little attention the editorial tradition has paid to the fact of a drama that speaks in this way—few commentators get beyond Pafford's observation that "the speech is meant to be incoherent": that is, Leontes is crazy, and his language is an index to his character.[5] The problem with this is not merely that it commits the play to the imitative fallacy, but that this sort of linguistic opacity is not at all limited to Leontes. Hermione, Camillo, Antigonus, and Polixenes all exhibit it on occasion as well. It is a feature of the play.

III

What does it mean that a drama speaks incomprehensibly? Even if we were persuaded that we had successfully elucidated all a play's obscurities, no actor can speak meaning rather than words, and no audience, least of all Shakespeare's in 1611, comes supplied with the necessary notes and glosses. Of course, we assume that we are, by elucidating, recovering meaning, not imposing it; but is this assumption really defensible? How do we know that the obscurity of the text was not in fact precisely what it expressed to the Renaissance audience? Is meaning, in any case, a transhistorical phenomenon? To take only a single famous example, the history of interpretations of the phrase *ut pictura poesis* in Horace's *Ars Poetica* would suggest that it is not.[6] The phrase for us is quite unambiguous: Horace says that poems, like paintings, have various ways of pleasing, some by detail, some by their broad sweep. Nothing in the Horatian context appears to us to admit the standard Renaissance interpretation, that poetry should be pictorial. Our interpretation is plain common sense; the Renaissance version is strained and illogical, wrenching the phrase from its context, "contaminated," as we would say, by Simonides's equally famous dictum that poetry is a speaking picture, with which Horace's phrase was usually equated.

Clearly, however, there is nothing common about common sense, which is as culturally specific as anything else in our intellectual lives. Renaissance strategies of interpretation call into question our axiomatic assumption that a plain prose paraphrase is the bottom line in unlocking the mysteries of an occluded text. If we look at what gets elucidated in the marginal glosses and footnotes of Renaissance editions, the idea that we are *recovering* meaning by looking up hard words and sorting out syntax becomes very difficult to maintain. E. K.'s glosses to *The Shepeardes Calender*, for example, deal with sources and analogues, but they seem designed primarily as a legitimating strategy for what is being presented as a radically new kind of text. E. K. very occasionally undertakes to explain a hard word, which is invariably conceived to be hard only because it is archaic. Syntactical and conceptual matters are not dealt with at all. The reason may, of course, be that to the sixteenth-century reader they were clear enough (whatever "clear" meant to such a reader); but it may also be that in some different and much larger way they were not felt to be problematic, so that their complexities and obscurities were, for the commentator, a part of the meaning, not to be removed by elucidation.

In this respect the claims of Spenser for the "dark conceit" of the *Faerie Queene* and of Chapman and Jonson for the virtues of the mysterious in poetry may be less uncharacteristic of the age than our construction of literary history has assumed.[7] The glosses of the great sixteenth-century humanist editions of the classics exhibit a similar pattern: historical, ethical, and philosophical commentaries, cross-references, analogues, and sources fill the margins. Confusions or solecisms are dealt with only as part of the editorial process, by emendation, usually silent—such matters certainly bear on interpretation, but they are considered prior to elucidation. Obscurity, or perhaps obscurantism, had by 1607 begun to be an issue primarily in legal texts, as the publication of John Cowell's *The interpreter: or booke containing the signification of . . . such words and termes as are mentioned in the lawe writers or statutes* testifies.[8] It also testifies to the dangers of elucidation: the book was suppressed by royal command because of its absolutist interpretation of such terms as *prerogative* and *subsidy*, an interpretation that the king would certainly not have found unsympathetic, but that was, for precisely that reason, better left a mystery.

IV

But in the largest sense, all this is largely irrelevant, an answer to the question of how a Jacobean commentator would have glossed a Shakespeare text. The idea is not inconceivable—Jonson, after all, annotated a number of his plays and masques—but that was part of a systematic reconceiving of the theatrical as textual, the transformation of scripts into books, and, moreover, into classics. Jonson's folio of 1616, with its novel (and, to a number of his contemporaries, ludicrous) claim that plays were "works," provided the essential model not only for the Shakespeare folio but for the subsequent editorial treatment of the Shakespeare canon. In this form the play became a transaction between the author and the reader, enabled and mediated by the editor. What this conception of the play omits is precisely what Jonson wanted to omit: actors and audiences.

When the audience first sees the actor playing Polixenes in *The Winter's Tale*, he is required to tell Leontes,

> I am question'd by my feares, of what may chance,
> Or breed upon our absence, that may blow
> No sneaping Winds at home, to make us say,
> This is put forth too truly (1.2.12–15)

Warburton declared this "nonsense," but doubtless a sense can be got out of it. Shakespeare had *something* in mind, and editors since the late eighteenth century have invariably assumed that this something must have been a paraphrasable meaning, which it is their task to recover. The problematic part of the passage, "that may blow/No sneaping Winds," etc., is generally glossed more or less as follows: "so that no destructive events may arise at home to persuade me that my fears were only too well founded." Some editors take "that" to imply a wish rather than a contingency and gloss the line "*oh* that no biting winds," etc. The passage has, over the centuries, suffered much inconclusive elucidation.

Polixenes obviously wants to go home, but his reasons are elliptical and obscure, and his metaphor changes in mid-sentence. The kingdom is conceived as a garden; with the gardener-king absent, the plants have no protection against the "sneaping winds," whatever these may be. Attempts to make "This is put forth too truly" part of the same metaphor have resulted in outright revision and paraphrases that wander very far from the text: Hanmer changed "truly" to "early," understanding "put forth" to imply the unseasonable appearance of buds. Some editors have adopted this, but it makes the relevance of the metaphor even more obscure. Quiller-Couch and Dover Wilson, who thought Hanmer's emendation was "probably right," saw the sneaping winds as Polixenes's response to some conspiracy he fears is breeding at home and which, were he on the spot, could be nipped in the bud.[9] Pafford wanted Polixenes's fears to be tormenting him precisely "in order that no biting winds may indeed blast affairs at home."[10] And so forth.

Such interpretations strike me as excessively arbitrary, though of course there is no way of determining whether they are right or wrong; and if it is really the sensibility of Shakespeare we are concerned with, it is difficult to see what alternative there might be to addressing linguistic problems in this fashion: the playwright must have meant something. But in a larger sense we are not, or at least not only, concerned with Shakespeare's mind. Plays may start as private musings, but they then become scripts performed by actors for spectators, and their ultimate success depends on what they convey to those spectators. What did an audience hearing the speech in 1611 think it meant?

What does an audience think it means now? Moreover, we need to remember that the Renaissance tolerated, and indeed courted, a much higher degree of ambiguity and opacity than we do—we tend to forget that Shakespeare's age often found in incomprehensibility a positive virtue. The discontinuity between image and text in Renaissance iconographic structures has in recent years, largely through the work of Erwin Panofsky and Edgar Wind, become a commonplace. Symbolic imagery was *not* a universal language; on the contrary, it was radically indeterminate and always depended on explanation to establish its meaning. When the explanation was not provided, as was generally the case, the spectators remained unenlightened. But this was not a problem: "no doubt," as Ben Jonson put it, "their grounded judgements did gaze, said it was fine, and were satisfied."[11] This particular observation described the response of uneducated spectators to an elaborate civic pageant, but even writing for an intellectual elite, Jonson strove for what he called "more removed mysteries,"[12] and his printed texts included explanatory commentaries designed, as he put it, finally, months or years after the event, "to make the spectators understanders."[13] The satisfaction in such cases derived precisely from the presence of the mystery, which assured the audience at abstruse spectacles, whether groundlings or scholars, that they participated in a world of higher meaning. We are familiar with such strategies in court masques, but they are also not alien to popular drama. *Pericles*, which Jonson attacked for pandering to popular taste, includes a procession of knights bearing symbolic shields and mottos that require elucidation to be understood, but which are not elucidated.

As editors, we all subscribe, however partially or uncomfortably, to some version of Jacob Burckhardt's Renaissance, an integrated culture that still spoke a universal symbolic language. For theater historians this view of the period was, or should have been, seriously compromised when Aby Warburg analyzed two of the learned spectators' accounts of the famous Medici *intermezzi* of 1589, probably the best documented of the great Renaissance festivals, and observed that the meaning of the performance, and the very identity of the symbolic figures, was opaque to even the most erudite members of the audience.[14] Since Warburg's essay was published in 1895, it is time Renaissance studies begin to take it into account; it bears on our general sense of the nature of Renaissance public discourse as a whole. The spectator of *The Winter's Tale* in 1611, we implicitly assume, would have understood it all. What we are now recovering, we tell ourselves, is only what every Renaissance audience already knew. I am arguing on the contrary that Shakespeare's audience was more like the audience constructed by Warburg than like the audience constructed by Burckhardt; that what Polixenes's speech conveyed to Shakespeare's audience is pretty much what it conveys to us: vagueness and confusion. It is clear that the king of Bohemia is insisting he must go home; if anything is clear about his reasons it is that they are utterly unclear, despite the attempts of three centuries of commentary to clarify them. (Even Hermione, shortly afterward, says in effect, "if he really wants to go home, let him say so clearly."[15]) How we interpret this obscurity—as a function of Polixenes's character, or of the Sicilian court, of the language of kings, of the complexities of public discourse, of the nature of stage plays them-selves in the Renaissance—is the real critical question, and it remains an open one. Shakespeare's text, characteristically, gives us no guidance on the matter. We do it wrong when we deny that it is problematic and has always been so, and reduce it to our own brand of common sense.

—(1990)

6

Two Household Friends

The Plausibility of *Romeo and Juliet* Q1

I should begin at once by confessing that I have not solved the problem of the relation between the first two quarto texts of *Romeo and Juliet*, though I do have some ideas about what is wrong with the several attempted solutions. I focus here initially on a small number of moments in Q1 that make a different kind of dramatic sense from the same moments in Q2 and that seem to me thereby to give us a rather different play as a whole. Then I turn to what happens when we take those alternative dramas into account in thinking about the play and undertake to produce out of them a coherent *Romeo and Juliet*. Throughout this essay, I am concerned with the larger question of what the relation is between the texts that have been preserved in the quartos and the folio and the play on Shakespeare's stage, and ultimately with the translation of those printed texts back into theatrical performances. I have worked with Lukas Erne's edition of Q1, to which I am indebted.[1]

For a long time the differences between Q1 and Q2, and the presumed defectiveness of Q1, were explained by invoking the concept of memorial reconstruction: Q1 was claimed to be a text put together by actors with deficient memories. But over the years the arguments postulating memorial reconstruction in Q1 looked increasingly tenuous; and they have now been effectively demolished by Paul Werstine and Erne, though both retain them to account for small individual moments.[2] But memorial reconstruction will not help with any of the problems I consider. Here is Erne's concluding summary of his argument about the relation of the two texts, which seems to me by far the best proposal, an elegant account of a very complex situation: "Shakespeare's original script as reflected by Q2 seems likely to have been abridged before the play reached the stage, but this abridgment accounts only for a portion of the divergences between Q1 and Q2, the omissions, but not the textual differences. While the latter seem partly a matter of memorial agency, it seems possible that small-scale authorial revision also contributed a share towards them."[3] I quote this first, because, as will become clear from a number of my examples, it seems to me in general right; but there are some interesting cases that it does not account for. My essay is not framed as a debate with Erne but as an examination of some puzzles that Erne's edition has got me thinking about. Needless to say, I have concluded that the situation is even more complicated than his complicated formulation allows.

Let us start with the Prologue, famously a sonnet—but only in Q2; in Q1 it appears as two quatrains and two couplets. Now: if Q2 is the prior text, and Q1 is a revised version for the stage, did the reviser not realize that the Prologue was a sonnet? If the reviser was Shakespeare, was there some reason for changing it and making it *not* a sonnet? Or is this, right at the outset, a bit of memorial reconstruction, with the reporter forgetting the first and third lines of a quatrain? All these explanations are obviously problematic; it seems much more likely that the revision went the other way, that Q1 at this point was the prior text, and the Prologue did not start out as a sonnet, but turning it into a sonnet was a bright second idea. Is there a point to its being a sonnet (or becoming one)? Sonnets do figure significantly elsewhere in the play, forming part of the action during the ball scene, where the lovers' dialogue is an extended sonnet, with an extra quatrain after the couplet—the first expression of their love is a sonnet, though the sonnet cannot quite contain what they have to say. (Bradin Cormack has ingeniously suggested that the extra quatrain is the beginning of a second sonnet, interrupted by the Nurse.[4]) That might suggest that making the Prologue a sonnet, introducing the love story with a sonnet, was an afterthought—perhaps considered ultimately a mistake, since it seems not to have remained in the text: the folio omits the Prologue entirely.

In both quartos the Prologue is printed in italics, but whereas Q2's Prologue is clearly part of the action, supplied with a speaker, Chorus, Q1's Prologue is printed to look like a prefatory poem. So, if Q1 is, as Erne puts it, as close as we can come to the play on Shakespeare's stage, the typography of Q1 at this point is undertaking to make the play into a book.

The two prologues prepare us for rather different plays. Q2 gives us the version that has become standard:

> *Two housholds both alike in dignitie,*
> *(In faire* Verona *where we lay our Scene)*
> *From auncient grudge, breake to new mutinie,*
> *Where ciuill bloud makes ciuill hands vncleane:*[5]

To begin, the dignity and the symmetry of the two families is stressed—they are "both alike"—and this initially seems to be an aspect of "fair Verona," one of the things that make the city decorous and beautiful. But then the dignity turns out to involve an ancient grudge, which eventuates in "new mutiny"—a developing process is implied, and line 4 describes a continuing state of civil war. "Civil," like "dignity," has unexpected double senses: "civil blood" could mean "natural courtesy," an aspect of the dignity that makes the city fair; but by the end of the line we see that it means just the opposite, "civic warfare." In line 5, the "loins" that give life to their children are "fatal," both death-dealing and ominous or fated, and the lovers are "star-crossed," doomed by the malignancy of their horoscopes. This bears on the question of where the ultimate responsibility for the tragedy lies—if the lovers are star-crossed, then the feuding families with their ancient grudge are star-crossed too: they are, we might say, genetically star-crossed. However badly the families behave in what is obviously a continuing tragedy, fate, the stars, and their horoscopes are responsible. The lovers are "misadventured, piteous," and their love in line 9 has a "fearful passage": they have bad luck, and we are to pity and fear for them—this is an Aristotelian view of the nature of tragedy, as the Renaissance understood Aristotle: misadventure in the plot, pity and terror in the response, but no hamarteia, no hero with a tragic flaw.

The play promised by the Prologue of Q1 is significantly different, so different that editors have more than once declared it nonsense:

Two houshold Frends alike in dignitie,
(In faire Verona, *where we lay our Scene)*
From ciuill broyles broke into enmitie,
Whose ciuill warre makes ciuill hands vncleane.

Is "household friends" even possible? What then would "civil broils" mean? Courteous disagreements that break into open warfare? Possible—maybe even nice: this gives us a progression, and no ancient grudge—it does look as if Q2 is a revision. The ancient grudge is referred to later in both versions of the play, but in Q2's preliminary summary it dominates and determines the action. In Q1 the households are friends; they move from "civil broils" to uncivil ones. Perhaps most significantly, it is only Q2 that anticipates the end of the civil strife through the lovers' death, promising if not a happy ending, at least an ethically more satisfying one. Was that really cut from Q1, not added to Q2?

What are we to make of the sudden move into the theatrical present in both texts, the reference to the two-hours' traffic of our stage? This is the only Shakespeare play that calls attention to the length of time its action is to occupy in the theater (*The Tempest* does note that its action is taking place in real time, though the amount of real time is unclear). But Q1 can be performed in two hours, whereas Q2 would take more like three. Does Q2 begin by artificially speeding up its action by making us expect a shorter play; or is Q2 a draft that expects to be cut by an hour in the process of being prepared for the stage? Is two hours even intended as a real estimate of the play's timing, or is it simply a way of saying how the time will seem to fly?

There is a second chorus-sonnet in Q2, and it constitutes one of the most baffling elements of the text. In Q2, the Chorus looks like part of an uninterrupted action. It comes at the beginning of what is in modern editions Act 2 (neither the quarto nor folio texts have act and scene divisions) and implies a passage of time and a series of secret meetings and stolen kisses between the first two acts—between, that is, the ball scene and the balcony scene. These two scenes, however, clearly proceed without pause: Romeo leaves the ball, eludes his companions, and climbs into Juliet's garden, where she is, on her balcony, for the first time, sighing her heart out for him. Nor can the Chorus be projecting future action; Act 2 is also continuous—the whole point is how fast it all goes, "too rash, too unadvised, too sudden," no time for secret meetings now or later. This chorus is impossible in the play as we have it. It suggests an earlier version of the play more directly based on its source in Arthur Brooke's *Romeus and Juliet,* in which the wooing does cover several months—it may be relevant that the Prologue to Brooke's long poem is also a sonnet. The second Chorus is almost invariably omitted in performance, since it contradicts the action (though it was included in the 1954 Renato Castellani film, with John Gielgud, made up as Shakespeare, reading it from what must be an advance copy of the first folio). It has no parallel in Q1, though it is, oddly, retained in the folio text. Does its presence in Q2 and the folio merely indicate the desire for another sonnet? It does remind us, in any case, that the texts of plays are not the plays and that reading a book is different from going to theater.

Even at this preliminary point, the problems I have with Erne's summary are evident: establishing priority between Q1 and Q2 is not a straightforward matter. Q2 retains bits of what must be a plan for the play that was subsequently abandoned but also includes bits that look like sophistications and fine-tunings of Q1—there will be several more instances as I proceed. Q1 in turn in many places is clearly an edited or cut version of the text in Q2. Each of the texts is in some respects prior to the other. Complicating the situation is the fact that the manuscript behind Q2 was apparently defective in scenes 2 and 3, for which Q1 was used as the copy text. We do not at all know, however, that the problems with the manuscript were limited to this section, and additions, adjustments or revisions may have been required (or simply felt to be desirable) elsewhere as well. This script is being turned into a book; there is no reason, moreover, to assume that the reviser was Shakespeare.

Now consider the opening action. The play that has begun with a measured formal prologue at once becomes an exchange of insults between household servants and then a brawl. Benvolio, a Montague, enters and undertakes to keep the peace, followed immediately by Tybalt, a Capulet, who starts fighting. In Q2 Benvolio's behavior is in character with the meaning of his name, good will. In Q1, however, he *does not* try to keep the peace; he simply starts fighting with Tybalt. This seems more likely to imply a cut than to mean that Shakespeare subsequently, belatedly decided to make capital out of his name. Officers and citizens enter, then Old Capulet and Old Montague, with their young wives trying vainly to restrain them. And finally the prince, Escalus—"balance," as in the scales of justice, but also the scale recalls the symmetrical households, "both alike in dignity" and in enmity: equivalence can imply both tension and rest. The prince aborts the fight and carries off old Capulet. Old Montague asks what happened, and Benvolio's account of the quarrel is much more forthcoming in Q2 than in Q1, where he scarcely makes a gesture toward answering Montague's question—this again seems likely to indicate a cut to speed up the action, but like the cut in Benvolio's role at the beginning of the scene, it results in a significant change in his character.

Now Romeo: he is discussed before he appears. There are no cuts in Q1's version of Benvolio's speech here. Romeo enters, characterized through a dialogue that dramatizes the standard conventions of the sonnet—Romeo is established immediately as a passionate but thoroughly conventional lover. There are, however, some curious things—curious because if Q1 *is* a cut text, it is also a revised one, and things one would expect to be revised are left alone. For example, Benvolio has claimed, both to Romeo's father and again here, that he doesn't know what is ailing Romeo, and he now extracts the information that Romeo is in love. Benvolio asks with whom, and Romeo goes through an extended paean to his beloved's chaste unobtainability but pointedly refuses to name her. Nevertheless when in the next scene the list of invitees to the Capulet party is produced, Benvolio seeing Rosaline's name on the list knows at once that she is the woman in question. To make sense of this, you have to invent a continuation of their conversation while they are offstage at the beginning of scene 2, during which Benvolio extracts Rosaline's name. This quite changes the dynamic between Benvolio and Romeo; it also gives us a sense that there is a lot going on in the play that we are not being told. Is that deliberate? Or shall we simply say that this all goes by so quickly in the theater that we don't notice it—that the book is not the play? (Of course, most of what editors trouble themselves about is unnoticeable in the theater.)

Let us pause over the list of guests Capulet has invited to the ball:

Signor Martino and his wife and daughters;
County Anselme and his beauteous sisters;
The lady widow of Vitruvio;
Signor Placentio and his lovely nieces;
Mercutio and his brother Valentine;
Mine uncle Capulet, his wife and daughters;
My fair niece Rosaline and Livia;
Signor Valentio and his cousin Tybalt;
Lucio and the lively Helena. (1.2.64–72)

This is prose in both quartos and the folio, though it is quite regular pentameter and is now invariably printed as verse. Rosaline's name comes late, in the third last line. Presumably Shakespeare included her because that is the only way to get Romeo to agree to go to the party, but the list also reveals something about her that we have not been told: she is Capulet's niece—this is in both quartos (at this point Q2 was being set from Q1, so if there was a second thought on the reviser's part we wouldn't know it—the folio text, however, is identical). Why suddenly make Rosaline Capulet's niece? If wooing a Capulet is such a problem in the case of Juliet, why is it not an issue with Rosaline? But perhaps it is; perhaps this casts some light on Rosaline's refusal to be wooed—Romeo calls her imperviousness to him a devotion to chastity, "She won't be hit by Cupid's arrow," making her a conventional sonnet heroine; but is it perhaps instead a quite sensible recognition that romance with the family enemy is a bad idea?

This might open up a whole backstory, in which Romeo is compulsively drawn to the enemy, a romantically suicidal streak: he is doomed not by the stars but by his perverse romantic tastes—he says it himself, viewing the aftermath of the fight at the opening, "Here's much to do with hate, but more with love." The two have everything to do with each other, are aspects of each other. The Italian source for the play, one of Matteo Bandello's *Novelle* (1554), includes an overt version of this hypothetical backstory: in Bandello, Romeo proposes marriage to Giulietta precisely as a way of ending the feud between the two families. The romance is public, and political, and it is defeated by the older generation's refusal to go along with this resolution of the conflict, the continuing wish for reciprocal revenge. This was the basis for Bellini's brilliant opera *I Capuletti ed i Montecchi*, which has nothing to do with Shakespeare, but as a way of viewing the plot it serves as a powerful commentary on the play, opening up its very private world to its very public implications.

Returning to the list of invitees to the ball, we notice, right in the middle of line 5, that Mercutio is also on it. Capulet has said this is a list of people he loves. Mercutio is Romeo's best friend. What is Mercutio doing there? Editors make nothing of this, but surely it ought to pull us up short, just as short as learning that Rosaline is Capulet's niece. At the very least, it indicates that the two sides in the quarrel certainly are not clearly defined. It starts to look as if Q1's "Two household friends alike in dignity" might not be wrong. "From civil broils broke into enmity"—civil in the context of "friends" needs much less explanation than it does in the context of ancient grudges. If we consider the guest list, the play is not about inveterate enmity but about friends becoming enemies and enemies becoming lovers. Here's much to do with hate, but more with love.

It hardly needs to be added that one becomes aware of all this only as one reads the play. Performances allow no time for such questions; plays are not books. But this play has become a book (or really, two books, followed by a proliferating series of derivations). Nevertheless, the printed texts are, after all, versions of the original scripts. The questions I am posing bear not on the effect of the play in performance—on what the audiences saw—but on what the actors had to work with: on the nature of those scripts and therefore ultimately on Shakespeare's imagination. It is worth adding that one characteristic of Shakespeare's imagination, in play after play, was a love of red herrings.

The play is built around set pieces: Romeo's opening account of his hopeless love; the Nurse's reminiscence of the earthquake; the Queen Mab speech and Mercutio's obscene conjuration of Romeo; the expanded sonnet in the ballroom scene; the balcony scene; Friar Laurence's Act 2 soliloquy and meeting with Romeo; Juliet's "gallop apace" speech; Juliet's potion speech; Romeo's speech in the tomb; Friar Laurence's interminable concluding summation; and of course the opening Prologue and Q2's inaccurate and superfluous introductory sonnet to Act 2.

The Queen Mab speech (1.4.53–95) is one of the play's great moments, though a curious point about it is how detachable this great moment is: it is nothing but a performance. It does not advance the plot, and even Romeo objects to its inclusion in the scene—"Peace, peace, thou talk'st of nothing." It is eminently excerptable, though marginally less so in Q2 than in Q1, since Q2's version is interrupted by Romeo in the middle of a sentence.

I want to focus on some tiny moments in the speech. Here is the opening in the two quarto texts.

> *Ben.* Queene Mab whats she?
> She is the Fairies Midwife and doth come
> In shape no bigger than an Aggat stone
> On the forefinger of a Burgomaster,
> Drawne with a teeme of little Atomi,
> A thwart mens noses when they lie a sleepe. (Q1)

> *Mer.* O then I see Queene Mab hath bin with you:
> She is the Fairies midwife, and she comes in shape no bigger thē
> an Agot stone, on the forefinger of an Alderman, drawne with
> a teeme of little ottamie, ouer mens noses as they lie asleepe: (Q2)

Two things are immediately noticeable: in Q1, the speech is spoken by Benvolio. The subsequent dialogue makes it clear that this is incorrect, that what has happened is that Mercutio's speech prefix has been omitted; but the usual explanation, that the compositor was pressed for space, clearly is wrong: the first line of the speech with a speech prefix would produce a perfectly manageable line, not even as long as Mercutio's line above it. It does look as if the compositor thought the speaker was Benvolio, which is not unreasonable, since in Q1 Benvolio is present throughout the dialogue.

But now consider Q2. Benvolio's question has disappeared, and the conversation is now entirely between Mercutio and Romeo—Benvolio is present in the scene, but he has been eliminated from this part of the dialogue. More strikingly, the speech is set as prose—this is obviously wrong; the speech is quite regular blank verse; and the final three lines, which begin the next page, are set as verse. The prose here may indicate no more than that Q2's compositor needed to save space on this page; however, it often is unclear in manuscripts whether a passage is verse or prose—the telltale uppercase letter to begin each verse line was on the whole not a manuscript convention, nor was the right-hand margin of prose always justified. But elsewhere in the play Mercutio does for the most part speak prose; to that extent, this is an uncharacteristic set piece for him, and Q2's typography is in character.

The Nurse's speeches offer an interesting, if confusing, parallel. Both quartos set her reminiscences, which constitute her big set pieces, in prose, though they are, like the Queen Mab speech, clearly blank verse. But the Nurse's speeches in her early scenes are also, in both quartos, set in italics, as if to indicate that what she speaks is not merely dialogue but a different order of discourse. A servant's speech at the end of scene 3 is also set in italics. Normally it is things outside the dialogue, such as stage directions or speech headings, that are set in italics. So are foreign languages, and written communications within the dialogue, such as letters, or Capulet's party guest list (which is referred to as a letter). The Nurse's later speeches are set in roman (and the folio sets all her speeches in roman), so whatever the italics imply, they do not distinguish her as a special kind of character—speaking with an accent, for example. But they do contribute to a continuous sense of indecisiveness or arbitrariness in the process of rendering performance as text, transforming the stage's dialogue into a book, as if the play is constantly eluding or confusing the typographer, who sets passages of verse as prose and passages of roman as italic, and gives a major set piece to the wrong character.

Return now to several tiny puzzles in Mercutio's performance, which are interesting because they are so curiously resistant to analysis. In Q1, Queen Mab is the size of an agate in a ring worn by a burgomaster—this is a measure of the fairy's smallness, but it also indicates a large agate, large enough to serve as an adornment to high civic office; a showy agate then. In Q2 the burgomaster is an alderman. A burgomaster is a civic official in a Flemish or Dutch town; alderman is the English equivalent. Neither, of course, has anything to do with Verona, but the domestication of the fantasy in Q2 seems worth noting—very literally domesticated in this case: Shakespeare's father was for a time the Stratford alderman and subsequently the High Bailiff, the equivalent of mayor. Aldermen, then, are familiar figures—our fathers, our neighbors—whereas burgomasters are foreign and to that extent exotic, and the Flemish and Dutch live well and like to show off. Does that part of the imagery translate into aldermen—were aldermen notoriously showy? Was Shakespeare's father? Did he sport an agate ring? Does this tiny change, if it was Shakespeare who made it, say anything about his attitude toward his father's eminence? Was he proud of it, or perhaps a little embarrassed by his father's performance in the role? By 1596, the date of the play, his father was bankrupt, accused of usurious and fraudulent dealings; he had resigned or been removed from all his public offices and had stopped going to church to avoid being arrested for debt. The year 1596 is also when Shakespeare revived his father's petition for a coat of arms, a declaration that, despite his reverses, he was nevertheless a gentleman. Is there any nostalgia in the passage? Which way did the revision go? The version with alderman is universally adopted now, and the change may be explicable simply as an editorial clarification. But perhaps the revision went the other way: did Shakespeare perhaps have second thoughts; did alderman involve a painful nostalgia or a deep family embarrassment, safely distanced by a change to burgomaster?

There is another strange small dissonance a little further on: in Q1, Queen Mab's wagoner is "Not half so big as is a little worm/Picked from the lazy finger of a maid." In Q2 the worm is "pricked from the lazy finger of a man." The change from picked to pricked is a change from bland and vague to vital and specific, which suggests to me that Q2's version is a revision. The change of the gender is more puzzling. Most of the figures assaulted by Mab in the speech are male—she drives over men's noses, through lovers' brains, over courtiers' knees and lawyers' fingers; but she also meddles with ladies' lips and presses maids when they lie on their backs, "Making them women of good carriage"—preparing them, that is, for men. The speech is largely a masculinist fantasy, hence, perhaps, the change from "picking" to "pricking" and the association then of pricks with men's fingers, not women's. Elsewhere, of course, Mercutio's language is notoriously phallic: "the bawdy hand of the dial upon the prick of noon"; the threat "to raise a spirit in his mistress' circle/Of some strange nature, letting it there stand/Till she had laid it and conjured it down": and especially the joke about "that kind of fruit/That maids call medlars when they lie alone," a joke so dirty that Mercutio's gloss, "O that she were an open—," where "open" is part of a word that lexicographers now assure us should have been "open-arse," a slang term for the medlar, was rendered by Q1's compositor "open etcetera," and by Q2's "open, or" (so that the line reads "O that she were an open, or thou a poprin pear").

Q1's "open etcetera" assumes we are all in on the joke; Q2 retains the smut but makes it both vague and part of a pair of genuinely pointless alternatives: O that she were an open anything, just woman defined by her openness to penetration—and this is presented as counterfactual, O that she were, if only, *magari*. But then, the fantasy continues, alternatively, O that *you* were a phallic fruit, the poppering pear. A poppering pear is a normal-shaped pear, with its phallic implications; the medlar has a soft cavity at its center. As a pair of alternatives, Q2 presents an image of pure frustration; without the open whatever, the phallic fruit has nothing to penetrate: the poppering pear cannot be an *alternative* to the medlar; the point is that they fit together. Editors assume a misreading of something by Q2's compositor, but it is clear that Q2's printer simply didn't get the point (whereas Q1's compositor knows exactly what he is doing). In any case, Q2 loses the wit. Both readings register discomfort, or even embarrassment; the page has a decorum that is not incumbent on the stage. If open-arse is what Mercutio said, the joke in the theater was not only bawdy but sexually polymorphous, with the identification now of the mistress's "circle" with any receptive anus.

To return to the worm that is "pricked," rather than "picked" from the finger, in Q2 it comes from within the digit; in Q1 it is merely picked off it—the sexual implications this time are clear enough (things *come out of* pricks), and they point to masculine sex, though in this case the sex is solitary, masturbatory; hence perhaps the additional implication that laziness, whether in men or women, breeds only worms, in the body or out of it. All this of course goes by so fast in the theater that none of these issues arise—that is, we are being told more than we can apprehend; we miss a lot, necessarily: it is too sudden, too like the lightning. The book slows us down so we can savor the poetry, but it also makes heavy weather out of wit that on stage is mercurial (or Mercutial).

Now let us consider another set piece, Juliet's soliloquy "Gallop apace you fiery-footed steeds" at the beginning of Act 3 scene 2. In Q2 this is a major soliloquy, thirty-one lines long. In Q1 it is all of four lines. Here are the whole speech in Q1 and the opening of the speech in Q2. Though it is natural to assume that Q1 must be a cut text to speed things up on stage, the parallel lines in Q2 look like a revision:

> Q1   Gallop apace you fierie footed steedes
> To *Phoebus* mansion, such a Waggoner
> As *Phaeton,* would quickly bring you thether,
> And send in cloudie night immediately

versus

> Q2   Gallop apace, you fierie footed steedes,
> Towards *Phoebus* lodging, such a wagoner
> As *Phaetan* would whip you to the west,
> And bring in clowdie night immediately.

"Whip you to the west" has more snap than "quickly bring you thither" and works better with "Towards Phoebus' lodging" than with the more specific and localized "To Phoebus' mansion." Q2 gives a direction and an action, Q1 a destination and a conclusion. And since twenty-five lines later Q2's Juliet says, "I have bought the mansion of a love/But not possessed it," this would be a reason for Phoebus' mansion to be revised out of line 3 in a later version of the speech. But did Juliet not originally have this sensational set piece, or was it not a part of the play on the stage? It includes many of the play's most famous bits: "Lovers can see to do their amorous rites/By their own beauties"; "Come, civil night,/Thou sober-suited matron all in black,/And learn me how to lose a winning match"; "Come night, come Romeo, come thou day in night"; and a seriously problematic one, "Give me my Romeo; and when I shall die,/Take him and cut him out in little stars,/And he will make the face of heaven so fine,/That all the world will be in love with night." Q4 (1622) changes "when I shall die" to "when he shall die," but all other early texts, including the folio, read "when

I shall die."[6] Editors in the past regularly corrected "I" to "he." Recent editors, however, including Jill Levenson in the Oxford edition, retain "I," citing the ambiguity in "die," the common Elizabethan term for an orgasm. Levenson does not, however, explain how to interpret the passage. Can Juliet really be imagining Romeo dead, diced, and stellified in order to celebrate her first orgasm?

As an anticipation of the wedding night this set piece would seem to provide a critical romantic context. Juliet's character deepens and matures in it (and, if "when I shall die" is right, reveals an interestingly kinky side). It is difficult to imagine the performers wanting to truncate it, though perhaps that is the view of a reader who has lingered over the poetry—we cannot imagine it cut simply because it is so familiar. Similarly, Juliet's big final set piece, the potion speech, a piece of bravura melodrama, is far shorter in Q1 than in Q2, seventeen lines as against forty-three. Here again one suspects both cutting in Q1 and revision in Q2; but if Q1 is the play on the stage, weren't these show-pieces precisely what audiences came to hear? Perhaps in another kind of play they were; but speed is of the essence in this tragedy of accidents, and lingering over poetry is a luxury best indulged by readers. The potion speech in modern productions is generally felt to be an embarrassment. In Franco Zeffirelli's famous film it was replaced by just four words, "Love give me strength." This was presumably all Olivia Hussey could credibly manage.

As for the larger issue of the dispensability of famous set pieces, the earliest Shakespearean promptbooks show just this sort of excision: the marked up copies of *Macbeth* and *Measure for Measure* in the first folio, now in the library of the University of Padua, consistently delete long passages of poetry—all Macbeth's big soliloquies are cut, all the big poetic speeches of Angelo and Claudio; these are passages that, for centuries of readers, have been what is most characteristically Shakespearean in these plays. But one can almost hear the stage reviser muttering "More action and less talk," and judging from Q1, this is how, from the beginning, Shakespeare moved from the page to the stage. So in the 1990 film of *Hamlet*, starring Mel Gibson, Zeffirelli was being authentically Shakespearean when he cut the "To be or not to be" soliloquy—this was a surprise and occasioned a good deal of criticism; but the biggest surprise for me was how well it worked, tightening the play and moving Hamlet toward what is, after all, the action we have been waiting for.

In fact, if *Hamlet* had not become such a canonical text we might realize that there are serious problems with the "To be or not to be" soliloquy. At this point in the play, surely "to be or not to be" is *not* the question; the question is revenge, an issue that is never mentioned in the speech. The question is also the reliability of the ghost that has commanded this dilatory hero to become an avenger: Hamlet himself wonders whether it is "a spirit of health or a goblin damned." But the speech ends by claiming that we resist suicide out of a fear of what we can never know, "the dread of something after death,/The undiscovered country from whose bourn/No traveler returns." If this speech were not so ingrained in our memories we would surely find it at the very least out of place, if not incomprehensible: Hamlet has just seen his father's ghost, who has told him what happens after death: the play opens with the traveler who has returned from the undiscovered country.[7] This speech would make sense only if Hamlet delivered it *before* he sees the ghost. In fact, a recent London production starring Benedict Cumberbatch did open the play with the soliloquy; but there were such howls of protest from the critics that the speech was moved back to its place in the familiar printed text. Actors have always revised plays to adapt them to changing conditions and new ideas (and in this case, to a really careful reading of the play); but in this instance the text had become sacrosanct.

Let us turn now to the ending of *Romeo and Juliet,* which the stage tradition has often found deeply unsatisfactory. In both texts Romeo arrives at the tomb too soon, finds Juliet apparently dead, drinks poison, and dies. Forty lines later Juliet awakes, sees the dead Romeo, and mortally stabs herself. Since at least the late seventeenth century the play has been revised to give the lovers a proper farewell scene. There was even claimed to have been a Restoration version in which the lovers survived—a happy ending—though this has disappeared. In Garrick's tomb scene, however, though both lovers did end up dead, they had an extended *Liebestod.* The text was taken from Thomas Otway's 1679 adaptation, *The History and Fall of Caius Marius,* which interpolated passages from *Romeo and Juliet* into a plot derived from North's Plutarch. As one reads the Otway play now, these moments seem basically parodic— Lavinia on her balcony sighs, "Marius, Marius, wherefore art thou Marius?" But Otway was perfectly upfront about the borrowings, and Shakespeare's original had no currency whatever on the Restoration stage—Pepys went to see the only revival, in 1662, and thought it was "the worst [play] that I ever heard in my life, and the worst acted."[8] In fact, *Caius Marius* was powerful and popular, and replaced *Romeo and Juliet* on the stage until Theophilus Cibber revived the Shakespeare text, more or less, in 1744. Even so, Cibber retained Otway's *Liebestod*.

There is an excellent account of the history of the play in the Restoration and the eighteenth century by George Branam, which I am relying on here.[9] Garrick produced the play in 1748, with the romantic lead Spranger Barry as Romeo. His prefatory note to the published version gives a good sense of the true afterlife of what seems to us Shakespeare's most perennially successful tragic romance: "*The Alterations in the following Play are few, except in the last act* [that is, in the tomb scene]; *the Design was to clear the Original, as much as possible, from the Jingle and Quibble which were always thought the great Objections to reviving it.*"[10] Jingle and quibble—so much for the famous poetry and wit. Tastes change, and theater is the great barometer of taste. For the tomb scene Garrick revised not Shakespeare but Otway—a farewell for the lovers was essential, but Otway's was too extended and didn't make enough of the tragic irony of the situation. So Garrick's Romeo takes the poison and then sees Juliet stir. For a moment both lovers are transported with joy, and Romeo only then recollects that he is about to expire, while Juliet, not understanding what is happening, says "there's a sovereign charm in thy embraces/That can revive the dead." They die on a moment of dashed hopes, a satisfactorily romantic end. This remained the play's conclusion on the stage for a century.

There is another element in Shakespeare's text that is really not recoverable on the post-Shakespearean stage, and that has to do with both cultural attitudes toward sexuality and with the conditions of Shakespeare's theater. Shakespeare's women were prepubescent boys. In Shakespeare's source, Brooke's *Romeus and Juliet*, Juliet is sixteen; Shakespeare reduces her age to thirteen, even insists on it (the Nurse recalls the date of her birth). This may be a nice metatheatrical touch reflecting the age of the boy playing the role, but it is also culturally significant in that Juliet has only just passed the age of consent, which in Elizabethan England (and until the eighteenth century) was twelve for women, fourteen for men. The age of consent is the age at which individuals can enter into a legally binding contract, in this case the contract of marriage; that is, this is the age at which children no longer require parental consent to marry, the age at which they may legally elope. If this seems to us unreasonably young, Paris, pressing his case as a prospective son-in-law, even claims to Juliet's father that "Younger than she are happy mothers made" (1.2.12). It is surely not the case that there were many twelve-year-old mothers in England—Paris may only be mirroring the Elizabethan envy of supposed Italian sexual precociousness—but in Shakespeare's Verona Paris cannot be far off the mark: Juliet's mother declares that she herself was fourteen when Juliet was born. And Romeo is in the throes of first love, with Rosaline and then with Juliet. For Elizabethans he would have been fifteen, the age at which, according to Renaissance physiology, males become sexually active.

The play, then, for Shakespeare's audience, was about a thirteen-year-old girl eloping with a fifteen-year-old boy—the romance of young love included a great deal to disturb audiences of parents with marriageable children in this patriarchal society. We inevitably miss this when the roles are played by mature, sexually secure, adults—in the 1936 film, Norma Shearer's thirty-six-year-old Juliet and Leslie Howard's forty-year-old Romeo did not seem preposterous only because the play was a classic and these were famous and glamorous stars— the play was not a play, it was a "vehicle," and all references to Juliet's age were removed. Two centuries earlier Theophilus Cibber's Romeo had as his Juliet his own fifteen-year-old daughter—her age was right enough, but Romeo was literally old enough to be her father. Garrick was a mature thirty-three when in 1750 he reluctantly first played Romeo; his Juliet, the Irish actress George Anne Bellamy, was twenty-three. The Baz Luhrman film with a teenage Claire Danes and Leonardo di Caprio did capture some of the youthful transgressiveness of the original; and Zeffirelli's Olivia Hussey and Leonard Whiting inhabited their roles beautifully, though there were long stretches of Juliet's part that were cut, presumably because they could not be played convincingly by a modern sixteen-year-old—to say nothing of a modern thirteen-year-old. How effective the play can be when Juliet is played as (though not by) a thirteen-year-old is discussed in my essay "Shakespeare all'italiana."

We all come to these plays as readers; no matter how many productions we have seen, our opinions about what is essential derive from generations, from centuries, of editorial and critical history. And as the case of the recent London *Hamlet* demonstrates, so do the productions themselves. If it is true, as Lukas Erne says, that Q1 of *Romeo and Juliet* is as close as we can come to the play on Shakespeare's stage, it has to be added that "as close as we can come" is not very close. The book is not the play, and many plays may be derived from the surviving texts of *Romeo and Juliet*, all of them different, and all of them *Romeo and Juliet*.

—(2016)

7

Getting Things Wrong

I am concerned here with a number of Shakespearean cruxes and with the way criticism and editorial practice have undertaken to deal with them, whether by elucidating them, explaining them away, or otherwise accounting for them. I begin with some problematic names and textual muddles, and conclude with a group of geographical puzzles. The examples are so various that it is difficult to generalize about them, but they do seem to represent something that we might call characteristically Shakespearean.

I begin with some names and places. Early in *The Tempest*, Ferdinand, identifying himself as the king of Naples, describes to Miranda the loss he has just endured:

> myself am Naples,
> Who with mine eyes, never since at ebb, beheld
> The king my father wrecked.
>
> *Miranda.*   Alack, for mercy!
>
> *Ferdinand.* Yes, faith, and all his lords, the Duke of Milan
> And his brave son being twain. (1.2.435–439)

The Duke of Milan referred to is Antonio, Prospero's younger brother, who twelve years earlier had usurped the Milanese throne and sent Prospero and

Miranda into exile and probable death. The fact that Antonio has a son will come as a surprise only to those who are familiar with the play. Prospero has already given Miranda an extended, often passionate account of their history full of a sense of his grievances against his brother, and even at this early point in the drama it is clear that the plot will revolve around family relationships. A brave son of Antonio as a contrast to his unregenerate father and a parallel to Ferdinand is just what we would expect.

But Antonio's son is never heard of again. How shall we explain this? Explanations have varied according to how much of a lapse one considers it, and, if it is a lapse, how far one wants to exculpate Shakespeare from having committed it. Lewis Theobald, who was the first to notice a problem, gave the first and simplest explanation, that Shakespeare changed his mind without changing the line. This begs a few questions, to which I shall return; but it is certainly unproblematic. J. O. Halliwell-Philips complicated the explanation with a touch of romance: the missing son is a remnant of Shakespeare's source, as he put it, "the old play or novel on which this drama is founded." The old play or novel, however, is an invention of Halliwell's—*The Tempest* is notoriously a play without a source. A curious syntactical explanation was proposed by John Holt in 1749: that "his" in "his brave son" refers to "the king my father," and that his brave son is therefore Alonso's son, not Antonio's: Ferdinand is talking about himself. Though the syntax makes this explanation just barely possible, the problems are obvious—Ferdinand would not refer to himself as "brave," and he knows that he has not suffered the fate he believes has befallen his father. Nevertheless, the argument has resurfaced from time to time. Johnson, though he glossed passages immediately preceding and following this one, did not comment on the elusive son. Coleridge proposed that Antonio's son was in one of the ships that got away—the problem here was solved by enlarging the play's geography, though Antonio's total obliviousness to the loss of his brave son was not part of Coleridge's story. Staunton looked around the play for unaccounted-for personnel and proposed that Antonio's son was Francisco; the problem, he declared, had been introduced by the folio editors, who instead of listing Francisco as such in the cast list "carelessly coupled him with Adrian as one of the 'Lords'." But Francisco's paternity is nowhere alluded to in the dialogue, and in Act 2 scene 2 Antonio contemptuously lumps him with the rest of his toadying followers. The folio editors, we must conclude, were simply following the script. Staunton himself was not entirely persuaded and continued with an alternative possibility: "Otherwise, we are driven to suppose that to shorten the representation, the character as delineated by Shakespeare was altogether struck out by the actors, while the allusion to it was inadvertently retained."[1] So we are driven to conclude (who is driving us?) that the play was originally longer and had more characters, and these characters were ineptly cut: the culprits are now the actors, and Shakespeare in either case is in the clear.

Or not. J. Dover Wilson elaborated the argument and now laid the blame squarely on Shakespeare: Antonio's son was evidence of an earlier, longer, and far more circumstantial version of the play, beginning with the usurpation, which Shakespeare then revised and compressed, leaving some loose ends.[2] Frank Kermode, in his 1954 revision of his Arden edition, hazarded a very cautious speculation: "One hesitates to say so, but it looks as though Shakespeare began writing with a somewhat hazy understanding of the dynastic relationships he was to deal with, though he was certainly clear enough about the main theme of the play."[3]

What is this all about? Why didn't Theobald's simple common-sense explanation settle the matter? Why as late as 1954 did Kermode—not a critic known for caution in his aspersions—hesitate to imply that it just might be the case that Shakespeare hadn't quite finished thinking through the plot before he started writing, that perhaps the play hadn't sprung all at once full-blown from Shakespeare's head, with no second thoughts or uncertainties? Why the tiptoeing around the question? How had Shakespeare criticism become so hazardous, and what was Shakespeare being rescued from?

Critical editions tend to assume that every puzzle can be explained—the big surprise in the foregoing history of Antonio's son is Johnson's silence, which looks, in retrospect, like an admirable, if uncharacteristic, restraint. At a similar but more striking moment in *Othello*, the first time Cassio is mentioned he is described as "a fellow almost damned in a fair wife," but Cassio for the rest of the play is unmarried. At this crux, Johnson volubly threw up his hands, ascribing the missing wife to "corruption and obscurity" (a double culpability, then, the obscurity Shakespeare's, the corruption that introduced by his various executors). But for this kind of puzzle, it is difficult to see what sort of explanation there could be other than that Shakespeare changed his mind. The real question would be, then, the question that Theobald's explanation begs: If Shakespeare changed his mind without changing the line, how did these bits survive all the rehearsals and revisions, to remain a permanent feature of the text? And the answer about these two examples must be that they were simply too insignificant to bother with, like many Shakespearean inconsistencies, noticeable only to editors (and thus first noticeable in the eighteenth century), and in a larger sense, that no version of a Shakespeare play is ever a final version. The play is always a process, in progress; there is always unfinished business that any performance—or any edition—will undertake to complete as it sees fit.[4]

In fact, the editor's play is a very different matter from the actor's and, it has to be admitted, from the author's. In the cases of Antonio's son and Cassio's wife, the only credible elucidations assume an explanatory narrative about Shakespeare's mode of composition: he worked fast, he changed his mind, he didn't revise much. This sounds simple, but it does have implications for critics who want to see Shakespeare as always really writing for publication, always thinking of a final, canonical play. Editors can't afford such luxuries. For an editor, my simple narrative is often all one has to rely on.

I have written in the essay "Revising *King Lear*" in this volume about the moment in *King Lear* when Lear sends Kent off with "letters . . . to Gloucester," and then the letters become, in the rest of the sentence, a single letter, addressed not to Gloucester but to Regan (1.5.1–3), and I have discussed the editorial strategies for dealing with this and other textual puzzles in the play. I suggest in that essay that the process of composition and revision was unsystematic and piecemeal, in other words, theatrical: the muddles, then as now, go by quickly on stage; they pose problems only for editors and readers. Perhaps we misrepresent the plays by undertaking to elucidate everything. In one sense, we certainly do: there are, quite simply, some things in the texts of most plays of the period that the author was not clear about, and a lot more that even the original audience must have missed. Editors do experience and respond to and appreciate the plays they work on, but their experience is not the same as the audience's. It is, moreover, not quite the reader's experience either, because the editor's attention is directed toward errors and cruxes and muddles, precisely toward the kind of inconsistency I have been tracking. This is what editors do, what we need editors for, to sort out the muddles and inconsistencies, and at least account for the errors, even if they balk at correcting them, to get us through the cruxes and give us a clean, readable play. Even attentive readers are not obliged to think of the text as error in this way.

But if these muddles are simply, so to speak, an accident of composition, there are nevertheless confusions elsewhere in Shakespeare that my narrative about the playwright's creative process will not help with. For example, at the beginning of *As You Like It*, reference is made to Orlando and Oliver's middle brother Jaques, who is away at school; and then in the next act another character of some significance, also named Jaques, is introduced. Anyone seeing or reading the play for the first time will reasonably assume (as all my students do) that the Jaques of Act 2 is the middle brother, and it takes some time and some puzzlement and some attention to the cast list—which would not have been available to either Shakespeare's original audience or his original readers—to realize that this is not the case. When the original Jaques finally appears, near the end of the play, the other Jaques is onstage, and the speech headings, and the character himself, have to refer to the first one not by name but as "Second Brother" and "second son." This confusion seems utterly pointless, but is obviously deliberate; and one wonders how it survived the first rehearsal ("Will, can't we call him George?"). Similarly, in the *Henry IV* plays, a character named Lord Bardolph is introduced into Part 2, which already includes a character named Bardolph. No amount of elucidation will account for either of these, and my textual narrative does not get beyond the observation that for reasons that are not clear, Shakespeare introduced these confusions.

I now return to Theobald and a famous crux. The account of Falstaff's death given by Mistress Quickly in *Henry V* reads, in the folio text, "His nose was as sharp as a pen, and a table of green fields." This was the text from 1623 until 1726, when Theobald decided that Shakespeare's manuscript had been misread: that "a table of green fields," which seems to make no sense, was incorrect, and that instead, in dying, Falstaff "babbled of green fields."[5] This emendation, indisputably a stroke of editorial genius, seemed to have restored what Shakespeare must actually have written. Bibliography here communicated with Shakespeare himself—or at least, with Shakespeare's manuscript before it reached the printer.

But if we agree that Theobald was correct, and that a compositor setting the type in the printing house was misreading Shakespeare's handwriting, what happened before the play got to the compositor? "Table" is the 1623 folio's reading; so the folio's printer is the culprit. But the only other substantive text, the 1600 quarto, in a passage that bears little resemblance to the folio text, at this point reads not "babbled" but "talk"—Mistress Quickly says she heard Falstaff "talk of flowers"—and it is apparent that the folio was not set up from this very garbled quarto but directly from Shakespeare's manuscript. So neither of our two primary sources reads "babbled": "babbled," even if it is impeccably correct, is all Theobald. What then does the quarto tell us about the folio's crux? The quarto seems to be a reported text provided by two actors; but if the folio's "table" is a misreading resulting from a visual error in deciphering Shakespeare's handwriting, so would the quarto's "talk" seem to be. In a reported text, however, the error ought to be an auditory one. If the quarto is really a reported text, then, the counter-argument would have to be that the reporters heard "babbled" but remembered it as the simpler concept "talk" (or "talkd," as it is usually emended). This argument would be more persuasive if "talkd" looked less like "table." So has Theobald been perhaps too ingenious? Is "talked" the source for both "table" and "babbled"? Moreover, even if we agree that "babbled" was what Shakespeare wrote, it might also be the case that Shakespeare's handwriting was hard for everyone to read and was misread not only by the folio compositor but by the scribe who prepared the promptbook, who would also have been working from Shakespeare's manuscript—and the promptbook, after all, would have been the source of the actors' scripts too, and thereby of what the reporters heard, or misremembered. Maybe the actors were (incorrectly) saying "table" or "talkd" all along. For Theobald's purposes, however, what the actors said, what the reporters recalled, what all the audiences from 1599 to 1726 heard, was irrelevant; his communication was with Shakespeare's mind—or at least, with Shakespeare's bad handwriting. Theobald's intuition here effectively abolished both the performing and the textual traditions, the play's collective memory.

Surely the oddest thing about this sort of puzzle is to decide where the playwright fits into it. In 1599, Shakespeare was on the spot to see that the promptbook and the actors got it right—how could "table" (or "talkd") be wrong? Didn't Shakespeare thunder "'babbled,' not 'table,' idiots"; and why didn't the embarrassed prompter then immediately correct the error? How did the confusion survive the first rehearsal, to remain—like the second Jaques, Cassio's fair wife, Antonio's shipwrecked son, and Lear's letters to Gloucester—a permanent part of the play? And of course it has to be added that we do not know that they did: we really do not know what the relation was between what the actors performed and the manuscript that was given to the printer. The book is not the play.

Theobald's emendation of "table" to "babbled" has been acknowledged to be a stroke of editorial genius (I am not demurring), and his justification for it was enviably simple: the original made no sense. There are in fact paleographical difficulties with emending "table" to "babbl'd," but few editors have wanted to take them into account: the emendation, in my opinion, is almost certainly incorrect (if I were editing the play, I would print "talk'd," and nobody would be happy), but the attractions of sense over nonsense are very powerful, and babbled makes a much more attractive sense than talked. If Theobald's version was right, however, what was right about it has varied according to the various critical narratives it has generated. We all agree that there was no table, but why was Falstaff babbling of green fields? A decade before Theobald, Pope, in one of his more inventive editorial moments, had explained the table of green fields by declaring the phrase to be a stage direction that had mistakenly got into the dialogue: "This nonsense got into all the following editions by a pleasant mistake . . . A table was here directed to be brought in . . . and this direction crept into the text from the margin. Greenfield was the name of the property-man."[6]

Alas, poor Greenfield: once Theobald got rid of the table, the green fields required a different narrative. Theobald's story was that people who are near death and delirious with fever think about running around in green fields. Warburton scoffed: Falstaff by this time was not feverish, his feet were as cold as any stone, and running around outdoors would have been the last thing on his mind. Nevertheless, George Walton Williams, who has given an admirable survey of the genesis of this part of the editorial romance,[7] cites a number of very respectable critics, including Ernest Schanzer and Peter Ure, who have Falstaff imagining himself cavorting in the green fields of his presumptively pastoral childhood. For critics of the recent past, the most attractive explanation has had Falstaff turning to prayer on his deathbed, reciting the twenty-third psalm. No surprise here: the siren of intertexuality is especially hard for modern editors to resist.

The trouble is that the crucial line in every version of the psalm available to Shakespeare involves not fields but pastures, as it did a decade later in the Authorized Version, "He maketh me to lie down in green pastures." In Sternhold and Hopkins's Booke of Psalmes and the Bishops' Bible, moreover, the pastures are not even green but "pastures fair" and "pastures full." Did anyone in Shakespeare's audience hearing green fields think pastures fair or full? Or are we perhaps to assume, in an act of critical desperation, that Mistress Quickly, reporting Falstaff's dying words, heard pastures but remembered them as the simpler concept fields?

I turn now to a group of geographical cruxes. Shakespearean geography rarely coincides with the geography one finds in atlases and gazetteers, though the two occasionally intersect, sometimes tantalizingly, as when we learn that English players, including three who were to become Shakespeare's colleagues in the Lord Chamberlain's Men, performed at Elsinore in the 1580s. But for the most part Shakespeare's places seem to have little to do with real places, and indeed, in several striking instances even to conflict with them.

I begin with the most obvious and notorious example: in the middle of Act 3 of *The Winter's Tale*, Shakespeare lands Antigonus and the infant Perdita on the seacoast of Bohemia. In 1619 Ben Jonson made fun of Shakespeare's geographical ignorance, observing to William Drummond that "there is no sea near [Bohemia] by some hundred miles."[8] For over a century afterward there is no record of anyone else objecting to the setting, which also goes unremarked through the earliest eighteenth-century editions of Rowe, Pope, and Theobald. Hanmer in 1744 finally noticed Bohemia and declared it a "blunder and an absurdity of which Shakespear in justice ought not to be thought capable."[9] He duly rescued Shakespeare by emending the setting to Bithynia and blamed the folio's printers for misreading their copy. Subsequent editors were unconvinced and remained largely untroubled by Shakespeare's geography. The theater, however, was more receptive, and both Garrick's and Charles Kean's productions set the play's pastoral scenes in Bithynia—why geographical accuracy should have come to matter more on the stage than in scholarly editions is doubtless a question worth pondering. But we need to remember that "Bohemia" too is of the stage and must be what Shakespeare wrote: Jonson objected to the geographical solecism four years before the play's publication. Bohemia is what he heard in the theater, and the folio compositors were following their copy. The printers are in the clear.

Critics, however, intermittently continue to worry the issue and undertake to rescue Shakespeare from himself. Several (one as recently as 1955) have argued that because for brief periods in the thirteenth and sixteenth centuries Bohemia was part of the Austrian empire, it therefore did have a seacoast. This is like arguing that since 1850 Kansas has had a seacoast; nevertheless the claim still regularly reappears on the Shaksper internet forum. Most commentators have been content to explain the error away, as Pafford and Schanzer in their editions did, by observing that it is simply adopted from Shakespeare's source, Robert Greene's *Pandosto*. However, in Greene the kingdoms are reversed, and the seacoast is not in Bohemia but in Sicily.

H. H. Furness observed that there may, however, be a point to it: the Variorum cites three instances in which references to the seacoast of Bohemia are used to characterize a foolish or ignorant speaker, and S. L. Bethell argues on the basis of these that the setting was an old joke, analogous in modern times to references to the Swiss navy. He suggests that if W. S. Gilbert had included an admiral in the Swiss navy in one of his operettas, this would have been a good indication to a Savoy audience of how seriously to take the plot—*The Winter's Tale*, after all, declares itself a fairy tale.[10] We might agree with Bethell that the Variorum's examples settle the matter, except for the fact that Jonson didn't get the joke—how common could this commonplace have been? This may serve as a cautionary instance for our critical treatment of commonplaces—sentences beginning "Everybody in the Renaissance would have recognized" are usually untenable.

How real is Shakespeare's Bohemia (or as my students would put it, what is its ontological status)? More to the point, does this question have anything to do with geography? There is, to be sure, a place called Bohemia on the map, but is that the setting for the pastoral scenes in *The Winter's Tale*? Has it anything in common with the play's world? What associations would the geographical Bohemia have had for Shakespeare's audience—other than its lack of a seacoast, and apparently not all of them knew even that. They probably did all know that it was staunchly Protestant, but that fact seems entirely irrelevant to the play. The English edition of Ortelius's atlas, published in 1603, includes a map. It says of Bohemia what is clear from the map, that it is entirely surrounded by forests and hills (that is, it has no seacoast), and that "the ground is exceeding good for cattle and corn." A pastoral world then, at least? Not really: the Bohemians also mine metals and precious stones; and there are about eight hundred castles, towns and cities, of which the most noteworthy is Prague, on which Ortelius spends the rest of his account of the country, concluding that the populace "are greatly given to drunkenness, pride and pomp"—not a pastoral world at all, and nothing much to do with Shakespeare's sense of the place.[11] Presumably, then, he didn't look at Ortelius. But perhaps all this is irrelevant; perhaps maps are irrelevant, as they are in the case of that other Bohemia *La Bohème*. Puccini called his Italian opera Bohemia, in French, for reasons having nothing to do with geography. Puccini's Bohème is Paris and a certain kind of life one could live there. What is Shakespeare's Bohemia, if it is not a place on a map?

I propose that Shakespeare's Bohemia, with its seacoast, bears, and shepherds, is pretty much normative for Shakespeare's treatment of location. It is "elsewhere," but an elsewhere whose limits are set within the drama, not outside it. Why Bohemia, then, and not an invented name? Because this confrontational fairy tale is still part of our world; these kingdoms are not east of the sun and west of the moon. In fact, in Shakespeare it is the invented names that are anomalous: Portia's Belmont is unique. Locations may be vague—another part of the forest, a wood near Athens, a moated grange, an island somewhere between Naples and Tunis—but they are not nowhere. As for why Bohemia, why not? Who knows what associations the name had for Shakespeare? It has received an unusual amount of critical attention, but as a dramatic location it is in no way atypical. Prospero and Miranda, when they are expelled from Milan, are set adrift in a leaky boat. Critics since the eighteenth century have pointed out that Milan is not a port; counter-critics have argued that through a system of canals and rivers one could get from Milan to the Mediterranean by water (presumably accompanied that far by their captors: there would have been little point to setting them adrift in a canal). But if Bohemia can have a seacoast, surely Milan can be a port. The Messina of *Much Ado About Nothing* has no specificity at all, but Shakespeare does know that Sicily was a dependency of Spain, hence the presence of Don Pedro in a position of authority. It also, like the distant locales of many other Shakespeare comedies, has room for an unquestionably English clown, Dogberry, and the mysteriously Anglicized villain, Don John, and comprimario, Benedick. The Vienna of *Measure for Measure* has much in common with the London of Shakespeare's time and almost nothing in common with the capital of the Holy Roman Empire beyond its Roman Catholicism; but for the purposes of the play, that element is sufficient. There is no local color to identify the Athens of *A Midsummer Night's Dream* as ancient Athens, or the Verona of both *The Two Gentlemen of Verona* and *Romeo and Juliet* as anything other than a fictional place—Shakespeare clearly liked the name and the source stories; and for all the rich sense of detail in *The Merchant of Venice*, its topographical specificity does not extend beyond five allusions to the Rialto, which Shakespeare, like all American tourists, thinks is the name of a bridge, rather than the name of the district in which the bridge is located. Certainly both its financial dealings and its maritime economy suggest as much about London as about Venice, and at least one recent critic has noted that the name Shylock is unambiguously English, not Hebrew or Italian.

Consider Illyria, the setting for *Twelfth Night*. Shakespeare's principal source for the play, Barnabe Riche's story of Apolonius and Silla, takes place in Damascus.[12] Why did Shakespeare change it to Illyria? An informal survey of Shakespeareans several years ago determined that a significant number believed Illyria was a fictional place, like Belmont, and had no idea that for almost a millennium the name signified, more or less, the modern Croatia and Bosnia. There are, of course, reasons within the play for why this might be a natural, if ignorant, assumption—the play does not prompt you to look at a map, any more than Barnabe Riche prompts you to find out facts about Damascus. Nevertheless a conference on Shakespeare and the Eastern Mediterranean was convened in Dubrovnik in 2006, designed to set the record straight—two years earlier there had been a Catholic University conference on the same subject in the same place, but apparently there was more to be said. A Google search produces a substantial number of articles and lectures in the past twenty years on the rich cultural heritage of Dalmatia, many of which invoke *Twelfth Night*.

But is that what Shakespeare meant by Illyria? Here are some facts about Illyria. At one time or another it included much of the Balkans. In the sixteenth century it was variously subject to Turkey, Venice, and Hungary. Here is what the English edition of Ortelius's geography, which is exactly contemporary with *Twelfth Night*, says about Illyria: the coastal areas have better ports than the Italian coast opposite it, olives and grain are grown there, and there are excellent vineyards. The inhabitants were formerly much given to "robbing and thievery," but now are more civil and tractable. The most famous city is Ragusa (the modern Dubrovnik). Some political history follows, and Ortelius concludes by observing of the Illyrian province of Styria that it "nourisheth a people greatly troubled with an infectious scurf."[13]

What country, friends, is this? If you came away from seeing the play in 1603 and wanted to find out something about its setting, would any of this be relevant? Shakespeare must have had a reason for changing Damascus to Illyria, but was the reason geographical?[14] Countries are, in any case, not simply places on a map. They have demographies as well as geographies, and if Shakespeare's Illyria is Ortelius's Illyria, why is it populated by people with names like Orsino, Olivia, Malvolio—to say nothing of Sir Toby Belch and Sir Andrew Aguecheek? In fact, demography offers an odd connection between Shakespeare's Illyria and Shakespeare's Bohemia through Shakespeare's Vienna: the two prisoners in *Measure for Measure* who figure in the plot to substitute a head for that of Claudio are Barnardine, "a Bohemian born," and Ragozine, "a most notorious pirate"—though the latter's native Ragusa could, of course, be the one in Sicily. It is hardly worth adding that nobody in Shakespeare's Vienna has a German name.

Louise George Clubb, with whom I have been discussing the Illyrian question over many years, has proposed a provocative if distant set of interrelationships. There is in fact a connection between Illyria and at least the *Ingannati* tradition, of which *Twelfth Night* is a part—this is a literary connection, not a geographical one. The Croatian poet Marin Držić, who took his degree at the Sienese Academy in the 1540s and Italianized his name to Marino Darsa, upon his return to Ragusa/Dubrovnik wrote the most famous Croatian play

Dundo (Uncle) *Maroje*, performed in Ragusa in 1551—Clubb describes this as the first of the many adaptations of the *Ingannati* outside Italy. *Dundo Maroje* is not much like *Twelfth Night*, and Shakespeare certainly was not aware of it, but it includes disguises and deceptions, and though there are no twins, a cross-dressed woman figures prominently in the plot. It is a prodigal son story: Maroje has entrusted a large sum of money to his son, whom he has betrothed to a local girl and sent to Ancona and Florence to do business and outfit himself for the forthcoming wedding. (The "Uncle" of the title is a generic term for an elderly man; the boy is his son.) But the boy instead has gone to Rome, a sink of iniquity, squandering the money and spending his time with courtesans. Maroje follows him there, to recover what money he can and attempt to reform the profligate. The fiancée also pursues him, disguised as a boy. The play is thus about Illyrians in Rome, and here the geography really does matter: if "why is Illyria inhabited by Italians and Englishmen?" is not a meaningful question about *Twelfth Night*, "what are Croatians doing in Rome?" gets to the heart of *Dundo Maroje*.

But now let us turn to some cases where geography does seem to matter. In *All's Well That Ends Well* Helena leaves her home in Roussillon, in southern France, to pursue her beloved but unresponsive Bertram to Florence. However, she claims to Bertram's mother, the Countess, that she is on her way to the shrine of St. Jacques le Grand, which is in Compostela, in northwestern Spain (3.4.4–7). A glance at a map reveals that Roussillon is roughly halfway between Compostela, directly to the west, and Florence, to the southeast—Florence is in the opposite direction from Compostela, but that seems initially to be the point: Helena's claim seems designed to cover her tracks and throw the Countess off the scent. If you wanted to follow her, you would be heading the wrong way if you went toward Compostela. When Helena gets to Florence, however, she continues to claim that she is on her way to St. Jacques le Grand, and the widow with whom she lodges says "You came, I think, from France," expressing no surprise. Other pilgrims to the same shrine pass the same way in the scene. Clearly in the play, the route from southern France to northern Spain is southeast via Florence. As Susan Snyder says in the Oxford edition, "the geography here represents either error or deliberate mystification by Shakespeare; a third hypothesis, that Helen uses the pilgrimage only as a cover for her pursuit of Bertram to a different place, must account for other pilgrims to St. Jacques who pass through Florence."[15] It must also account for the widow's reaction—that is, for her lack of one.

I have no solution to this puzzle, but in the play it does send you to a map. Its very specificity makes it matter. If it is mystification on Shakespeare's part, to what end? The baffling thing is how unnecessary it seems: all the Italian states were Catholic; all of them had a multitude of shrines. A pilgrimage to almost any Italian shrine south of Padua might reasonably pass through Florence—Assisi, Loreto, Rome. Why Compostela?

But the alternative assumption, that Compostela merely indicates Shakespeare's geographical ignorance, is complicated by a very similar example closer to home, in which an English audience might be expected to be familiar with the geography, and Shakespeare cannot have been ignorant of it. In 2 *Henry IV*, after the conclusion of the hostilities in Yorkshire with the disbanding of the rebel army, Falstaff is directed by Prince John of Lancaster to return with him to the court at Westminster. Falstaff asks permission to go via Gloucestershire, which Prince John grants without comment; Falstaff subsequently explains to Bardolph that he wants to see Justice Shallow, from whom he intends to borrow money. Now the road from Yorkshire to London runs pretty much straight south down the east side of England—Gloucestershire is a very large detour westward. If this is intended as a geographical joke about how far out of the way Falstaff is willing to go to cadge money from his old friends, Shakespeare has done nothing to set the joke up—in the play, Justice Shallow has not been located in Gloucestershire until just this moment. In the only previous scene in which he appears, Act 3 scene 2, no location is identified. Why not put him in Cambridgeshire, or Berkshire, or anyplace not so preposterously out of the way? In this case Shakespeare certainly knows his geography, since Gloucestershire is adjacent to his native Warwickshire; but Prince John asks no questions—perhaps he is just as happy to be rid of Falstaff for a good long while. Is this the joke, and is the audience expected to be in on it? Nothing more is made of it, but when Pistol brings the news to Falstaff and Shallow that the king is dead, Falstaff, preparing to speed to London to claim his place beside the new King Hal, says "We'll ride all night." The distance from Gloucester to London is 113 miles—three nights might do it;

perhaps two if you pushed the horses really hard. The puzzle would not exist if Shakespeare had put Justice Shallow in Walthamstow. It is surely intentional.

But perhaps neither of these examples has anything at all to do with geography. Perhaps they are just two more of the gratuitous confusions, red herrings and loose ends that Shakespeare, for whatever reason, liked. There is, however, one case where the matter of implausible distances and impossible journeys really does seem to function dramatically in a quite specific way. In Act 4 scene 1 of *Othello*, Othello is recalled from Cyprus to Venice because the Turks have been defeated, and Cassio is appointed in his place. The defeat took place only the day before—Othello arrives victorious from the battle just after Desdemona and Iago land, and that night is Othello's and Desdemona's first night together on the island and their first night together since their wedding; their lovemaking is interrupted by the drunken row staged by Iago. The emissaries recalling Othello arrive from Venice the next afternoon. This is totally implausible if one stops to think about it (which one doesn't): how long does it take for the news of the victory to travel from Cyprus to Venice, and then for the Venetian emissaries to travel back to Cyprus? The distance by sea is about 1600 miles each way. A really fast ship of the period had a maximum speed of seven knots, a little more than eight miles an hour—this is with everything working out right, good winds from the right direction, calm sea, perfect sailing conditions for the whole voyage in both directions. The absolute minimum time for this voyage in one direction would be nine days; the round trip would take almost three weeks, allowing for time in Venice to deliver the news, get new instructions, and replenish the ship.

We are taught by the history of theater not to question such conventions, and this is one of a number of moments that make us believe there is much more time in the play than the plot allows. So in this case there is a point to the geographical impossibility: the space of this geography defines the period of time when Othello believes Desdemona and Cassio are carrying on together, the time between Desdemona's arrival and the arrival of the emissaries to recall Othello to Venice. This is the theatrical space and the dramatic time for Iago's scheming—the elapsed time has in fact been less than a day, but the play's geography gives Iago, and as far as Othello is concerned, Cassio and Desdemona, a good three weeks. The geographical absurdity is, moreover, not a matter of error but of outright deception. The deception, however, is not being practiced on Othello by Iago; it is being practiced on the audience by Shakespeare.

I am aware that I have concluded with a number of examples that lead us nowhere, if what we want is a general statement about Shakespeare's knowledge and use of geography. But it must be relevant that with the exception of *The Merry Wives of Windsor*, none of the comedies and tragedies is set in a location that would have been familiar to either him or his audience. *The Taming of the Shrew* opens in his native Warwickshire (Christopher Sly mentions two villages near Stratford), but then the play presented for Sly's entertainment moves the action to Padua and the world of Italian farce, and never returns; Sly and Warwickshire disappear, and the play is *The Taming of the Shrew*, not *The Gulling of Christopher Sly*. This might be an epitome of how Shakespearean geography works and how the familiar is made to feel other. Falstaff and Hal hatch their plots in a tavern in Eastcheap, and there are very specific London histories, like *Richard III*, but there are no London comedies, and even Shakespeare's Forest of Arden is not the one in his native Warwickshire but the Ardennes in France. Ben Jonson, in contrast, was moving ever closer to home, setting the comedies after *Volpone* in London and even transporting the 1599 *Every Man in His Humor* from Italy to London when he included it in the 1616 folio. The London stage at the height of Shakespeare's career was increasingly localized; city comedy was the genre of choice, and the city was usually London. But Shakespeare's city comedy is *Measure for Measure*, set in a Vienna that both is, and is not, London. He looked elsewhere, to places that were seemingly particularized only as names on a map. And perhaps that is the point: his stage was another country.

In short, every crux generates a proliferating set of critical narratives. It will be observed that none of my textual narratives ends. They all constitute only beginnings to stories that their plays cannot complete and that the larger dramatic narrative often contradicts. But the muddles, the loose ends, the red herrings, are also part of the excess that makes Shakespeare so much more interesting than any other dramatist, and keeps us, always, trying to explain.

—(2011/2012)

8

Food for Thought

The banquet scene in *The Tempest* is one of a number of evocations of *The Aeneid* that re-enact the events of the crucial European epic of empire. Many of these allusions are ironic or subversive: the Neapolitans returning from Tunis argue over whether it is the ancient Carthage, and invoking "widow Dido" they implicitly declare Virgil's Dido a fiction; and Prospero, near the play's conclusion ventriloquizing Ovid's Medea, articulates the play's celebration of the power of metamorphosis and storytelling, as against conquest and dynastic rule. In Virgil, the shipwreck victims' banquet is immediately attacked by harpies, who render the food inedible. In Shakespeare the harpy is Ariel, and what he delivers to the hungry Neapolitans is only memory, couched in the severest moral terms. This is Prospero's banquet, revenge eaten cold. But the scene is also one of the most elaborate theatrical spectacles in the play, food for the eye, not at all disappointing or delusory for an audience.

Literary banquets more often than not include unpleasant surprises—the surprise is generally the point of the feast, as in *The Tempest,* tragic for the characters, but for audiences a satisfying climax to a theatrical meal. The chief classic models are the banquet Tantalus serves the gods, at which the meat is the body of his son Pelops; and the meal Pelops's son Atreus prepares for his brother Thyestes, at which Thyestes is served the bodies of his sons. The Atreus scene is refigured, rather perfunctorily, as the concluding act of vengeance in *Titus Andronicus*—perfunctorily precisely because the scene was a classic, and an educated Elizabethan audience already knew what Saturninus and Tamora were eating; moreover, for anyone without a classical education, Titus spells out his plan in advance. Feasts ending badly are also imperial foundation myths, like the feast offered by Romulus to his neighbors across the Tiber, which concluded, as it was intended to do, with the abduction of the Sabine women to populate the new empire.

Shakespearean dinners especially are rarely comforting and convivial. The meal offered by Petruchio to his bride on their honeymoon is a cruel tease, with course after course rejected over the protests of the starving Kate. The banquet prepared by Macbeth and Lady Macbeth for the visiting Duncan is served off-stage, an ironically festive background for a scene in which the hosts plan the murder of their guest; and at a subsequent banquet Macbeth is crowded out of his own table by the ghost of the murdered (and aptly named) Banquo. Antony and Cleopatra spar over who should invite whom to dinner; and then Antony, the guest, loses his appetite for anything except the sight of Cleopatra—the point of this banquet, obviously, was never the food. Timon of Athens belittles his feast—"there is an idle banquet attends you"—but then entertains his guests so lavishly that it is clear none of them will be able to reciprocate, or will wish to, or, when he is destitute, do. Capulet similarly unknowingly prepares his own downfall with his disingenuous invitation to the masked Romeo and Benvolio: "We have a trifling foolish banquet towards."

But what makes for a satisfactory meal? Prince Hal deplores the meagre proportion of bread to sack on Falstaff's shopping list; Hamlet has a similar complaint about the dining habits at his uncle's court. Lear complains that his dinner does not arrive quickly enough. Shylock refuses to dine with his Venetian clients—on religious grounds, to be sure, but it is doubtful whether he would be good company even at a kosher meal. Nevertheless, in George Granville's 1700 adaptation of the play *The Jew of Venice*, Shylock has definitively lost his qualms: business is business. He leaves Jessica with the words "I am bidden to supper" and is subsequently revealed dining with Antonio, Bassanio, and Gratiano, with a masque of Peleus and Thetis for entertainment. Shylock's conviviality is, to say the least, forced, though his religious principles are probably not in danger, since all the diners seem to be doing is drinking.

Toasts are proposed: Antonio drinks to friendship, Bassanio to love, Gratiano to women in general; and then it is Shylock's turn:

I have a Mistress, that out-shines 'em all—
Commanding yours—and yours thro' the whole Sex:
O may her Charms encrease and multiply;
My Money is my Mistress! Here's to
Interest upon Interest. [*Drinks.*]

Antonio is duly appalled:

Let Birds and Beasts of Prey howl to such Vows,
All generous Notes be hush'd: Pledge thy self, Jew:
None here will stir the Glass—   [*All Rise.*]
Nor shall the Musick sound: O *Bassanio*!
There sits a Heaviness upon my Heart
Which Wine cannot remove: I know not
But Musick ever makes me thus.[1]

Bassanio explains, "The Reason is, your Spirits are attentive," and so on to the
rest of the love duet that Shakespeare had composed for Lorenzo's reply to
the pensive and apprehensive Jessica near the play's conclusion. The masque
of Peleus and Thetis is then performed; Bassanio takes his leave for Belmont,
bidding a courteous farewell to Shylock, whose only response is an aside:

These Christian Fools put me in mind
Of my Money: just so loath am I to part with that[2]

(so loath, presumably, as they are to part with each other, not as he is to part
with them). An ominous feast indeed.

Ben Jonson's poem *Inviting a Friend to Supper* would seem to be the polar
opposite, promising nothing but good cheer. This most classical of Jacobean
poets issues his invitation by imitating an epigram of Martial:

Tonight, grave sir, both my poor house, and I
Do equally desire your company; . . .
Yet shall you have, to rectify your palate,
An olive, capers, or some better salad

Ushering the mutton; with a short-legged hen,
If we can get her, full of eggs, and then
Lemons, and wine for sauce; to these a cony
Is not to be despaired of, for our money;
And, though fowl now be scarce, yet there are clerks,
The sky not falling, think we may have larks.[3]

A handsome proposition; but are there hints even here that all may not be well? What is wrong with the guest's palate that it needs to be rectified? And though the disastrous possibility of the sky falling is obviously a joke, what is the point of the joke? And what are the clerks, experts, doing in the poem—will larks be on the menu or not?

Moreover, even this bill of fare seems to Jonson insufficiently tempting:

I'll tell you of more, and lie, so you will come:
Of partridge, pheasant, woodcock (17–18).

Jonson has Martial's authority for the lie:

I will deceive you to make you come: fish, mussels,
sow's paps, and fat birds of the poultry-yard and the marsh[4]

The real temptation here is not the food but the increasingly imaginative promise of food, acknowledged to be a fantasy: the lie, the deception, is the ultimate temptation, the fantasy that informs the poem, and makes the invitation irresistible. But there is more to dining than food. Jonson offers high-minded entertainment:

                    my man
Shall read a piece of Virgil, Tacitus,
Livy, or of some better book to us,
Of which we'll speak our minds, amidst our meat.

And even better, Jonson promises not to recite any poetry himself—including his own: "I'll profess no verses to repeat" (20–24). Martial had in fact gone him one better, inviting his poet friend Julius Cerialis to dinner—Cerialis was an imitator of Virgil and author of an epic on the battle of the Giants and the Gods:

> More I promise you: I will recite nothing to you,
> even though you yourself read again your *Giants* straight through,
> or your *Pastorals* that rank next to immortal Virgil.[5]

The irony here is obvious, though probably affectionate enough; Cerialis is expected to share in the joke. Jonson's tone is gentler, but surely less to be trusted, the notorious self-promoter promising for once to be modest. Is this simply a continuation of the lie about the food? Did Jonson have a reputation as a host who could be tedious? Here is James Howell describing supper with Jonson and his protégés in 1636, the year before Jonson's death. "there was good company, excellent cheer, choice wines, and jovial welcome: One thing interven'd, which almost spoil'd the relish of the rest; that *B.* began to engross all the discourse, to vapour extremely of himself, and, by vilifying others, to magnify his own *Muse. T[homas] Ca[rew]* buzz'd me in the ear, that tho' *Ben.* had barrell'd up a great deal of knowledge, yet it seems he had not read the *Ethiques,* which among other precepts of Morality, forbid self-commendation."[6] No doubt Jonson at sixty-three, ailing and stroke-ridden, was crustier than Jonson at forty; but perhaps by 1612 or so, the convivial host of the Mermaid already had an inkling that "to magnify his own Muse" was not the most welcome entertainment for guests. It is worth noting, moreover, what part of Martial's promise Jonson omits: that the guest may perform as much of his own poetry as he likes.

In Jonson's England, however, the tedium of a monopolizing host was not the greatest danger to be feared from a dinner invitation. Hence the final reassurance:

> And we will have no Poley, or Parrot by,
> Nor shall our cups make any guilty men. (36–37)

Poley is Robert Poley, a notorious espionage agent of the Elizabethan spymaster Walsingham, adept at posing as a Catholic, who had been instrumental

in revealing the Babington plot on the queen's life and had been present at
Marlowe's murder; Parrot is any spy who repeats what he hears. Jonson himself had been summoned before the Privy Council after Guy Fawkes's arrest.
He was by this time a Catholic convert, though he had not been implicated
by Fawkes; but he had dined with several of the conspirators at Robert Cates-
by's only a month before the discovery of the Gunpowder Plot and needed to
demonstrate his loyalty. He agreed to become a government agent himself, to
help entrap a suspect priest. Dinner invitations are dangerous; dinner conversation is revealing; conviviality can always be construed as conspiracy.

And of course there is also the danger that the guests may not like the
dinner. Robert Herrick's *The Invitation* is a disgruntled thank-you note, an
anti-type to Jonson's invitation, and a warning to hosts:

> To sup with thee thou didst me home invite;
> And mad'st a promise that mine appetite
> Sho'd meet and tire, on such lautitious meat,
> The like not Heliogabalus did eat:
> And richer Wine wo'dst give to me (thy guest)
> Then Roman Sylla powr'd out at his feast.
> I came; (tis true) and lookt for Fowle of price,
> The bastard Phenix; bird of Paradice;
> And for no less then Aromatick Wine
> Of Maydens-blush, commixt with Jessimine.

So far so good. But promises are cheap:

> Cleane was the herth, the mantle larded jet;
> Which wanting Lar, and smoke, hung weeping wet;
> At last, I'th' noone of winter, did appeare
> A ragd-soust-neats-foot with sick vineger:
> And in a burnisht Flagonet stood by
> Beere small as Comfort, dead as Charity.
> At which amaz'd, and pondring on the food,
> How cold it was, and how it child my blood;
> I curst the master; and I damn'd the souce;

And swore I'de got the ague of the house.
Well, when to eat thou dost me next desire,
I'le bring a Fever; since thou keep'st no fire.[7]

Doubtless Herrick's host had oversold his hospitality, as Jonson, in his poem, freely admits he is overselling his. Nevertheless, it can hardly have been only the food that accounts for the virulence of the disappointment. In fact, this is not an uncharacteristic poem; Herrick in the literary histories is far more good-natured and charming than he appears if we read through the whole of *Hesperides*. Nothing in the standard anthology pieces about Julia's clothes and petitions to fairies prepares us for the amount of barbed epigram and outright scatology in the volume—one wouldn't have encouraged Herrick to recite his verses over dinner.

Clearly for Jonson, but not for Herrick, the conviviality of a shared meal counts for more than the food. One could even say that for Jonson, the invitation alone counts for more than the dinner: the recipient was, after all, receiving the gift of a poem by a major poet. Hence the epicurean pleasures offered in *Inviting a Friend to Supper* are in fact relatively modest. In the imagined world of his drama, however, the fantasy dinners are far more inventive. Sir Epicure Mammon, anticipating his control of the philosophers' stone, conjures up the meals of his transformed life:

My meat shall all come in, in Indian shells,
Dishes of agate set in gold, and studded
With emeralds, sapphires, hyacinths, and rubies.
The tongues of carps, dormice, and camels' heels,
Boiled in the spirit of sol, and dissolved pearl,
Apicius' diet, 'gainst the epilepsy:
And I will eat these broths with spoons of amber,
Headed with diamond and carbuncle.
My foot-boy shall eat pheasants, calvered salmons,
Knots, godwits, lampreys: I myself will have
The beards of barbels served, instead of salads;
Oiled mushrooms; and the swelling unctuous paps
Of a fat pregnant sow, newly cut off,

Dressed with an exquisite, and poignant sauce;
For which, I'll say unto my cook, "There's gold,
Go forth, and be a knight." (*Alchemist* 2.1.89–104)[8]

When he is wooing Doll Common, Mammon's menu is even more elaborate:

we will eat our mullets,
Soused in high-country wines, sup pheasants' eggs,
And have our cockles boiled in silver shells;
Our shrimps to swim again, as when they lived,
In a rare butter made of dolphins' milk,
Whose cream does look like opals; and with these
Delicate meats set ourselves high for pleasure,
And take us down again, and then renew
Our youth and strength with drinking the elixir,
And so enjoy a perpetuity
Of life and lust! (4.1.198–208)

But Doll, even as she plays along, is a relentless realist. In the England of 1610, there are dangers in high living:

Dol. I could well consent, sir.
But, in a monarchy, how will this be?
The prince will soon take notice, and both seize
You and your stone, it being a wealth unfit
For any private subject.

Mam. If he knew it.

Dol. Yourself do boast it, sir.

Mam. To thee, my life.

Dol. O, but beware, sir! You may come to end
The remnants of your days in a loathed prison,
By speaking of it.

Mam. 'Tis no idle fear.
We'll therefore go withal, my girl, and live
In a free state (4.1.185–98)

The most explicit summary of the dangers of convivial dining comes from the misanthrope Apemantus, refusing to sup with Timon of Athens:

I scorn thy meat; 'twould choke me, for I should ne'er flatter thee.
O you gods, what a number of men eat Timon, and he sees 'em not!
It grieves me to see so many dip their meat in one man's blood; and
all the madness is, he cheers them up too.
     I wonder men dare trust themselves with men:
     Methinks they should invite them without knives;
     Good for their meat, and safer for their lives. There's much ex-
ample for't; the fellow that sits next him now, parts bread with him,
pledges the breath of him in a divided draught, is the readiest man
to kill him: 't has been proved. If I were a huge man, I should fear to
drink at meals;
     Lest they should spy my windpipe's dangerous notes:
     Great men should drink with harness on their throats. (1.2.38–55)

Apemantus's forebodings are preposterously melodramatic; Timon is never in this sort of danger from his guests. The worst he endures is ingratitude, which is certainly monstrous enough.

But transported into the context of *The Tempest,* Apemantus would be a realist: these are just the threats Alonso and Gonzalo unknowingly face from their banquet companions Antonio and Sebastian, who have already attempted to murder them in their sleep. Prospero's Virgilian performance for the shipwrecked Neapolitans is true food for thought, a delusionary banquet on an island where the choicest delicacies, the very best a dinner guest can actually hope for, are pig-nuts, marmoset meat, crabs (which all editors assure us are not the delicious crustaceans but only humble crabapples) and the incomprehensible scammels.

—(2017)

9

Revising *King Lear*

King Lear comes down to us in two versions, a quarto published in 1608, which seems to be based on Shakespeare's rough draft (that is, on the play before it was revised and cut to be performed) and the folio text of 1623, which is shorter and makes a number of changes, but is still too long to be the text that was performed. But then there is a significant subsequent history of revision, beginning in 1681, when the playwright Nahum Tate refashioned the play for the Restoration stage. The most notorious of his revisions was the ending: in Tate's *King Lear*, Cordelia's troops win the final battle, she and Lear survive, and Lear gets his throne back. This was the version of the play that was performed for the next 150 years: if you went to see *King Lear* in the eighteenth century, this is the play you saw. It has earned little but contempt from modern critics, who object to its sentimentalizing of this uncompromising tragedy; but the greatest eighteenth-century critic Samuel Johnson admired it, and that is where I shall begin.

Everybody agrees that Johnson is a great Shakespeare critic, but few of his observations can be as alien to modern sensibilities as his admission that because he found the conclusion of *King Lear* unendurably painful (a point in his favor, surely), he therefore preferred Tate's happy ending, because it both satisfied poetic justice and was true to history. The historical observation is correct, and is worth taking seriously: in all the sources, Cordelia's army is victorious and Lear reclaims his throne. It was Shakespeare who changed the ending, which would have surprised or even shocked the original audiences. Imagine a play about the American Civil War in which the Union is defeated, the south secedes, and slavery is not abolished—this is not true to history, but you could hardly leave it at that. It would give you quite a lot to think about: there was some point to the fabrication. So here I want to consider what Shakespeare's point was, in so clear a violation of his audience's expectations— expectations, moreover, that the play itself raises.

Tate's *King Lear* has had few admirers in the past two centuries, and to remark that it was the basis for the standard performing version of the play until well into the nineteenth century is only, for us, evidence of how perverse the theatrical tastes of the past are. I have a considerable investment in the original (or originals), having edited both the quarto and folio texts of Shakespeare's play, as well as—at the publisher's insistence—a conflated text, which consistently irritates me and vindicates the publisher by selling about five times as many copies annually. I propose here not to offer a defense of Tate (Johnson can take care of himself) but to consider the larger question of revision in relation to a history of retrospective readings of the Lear story, a history that must already have been in progress by the time the first quarto was published in 1608.

Historically, there has never been anything unalterable (or to use the usual loaded critical term, sacrosanct) about the text of Shakespeare, either for actors or editors. These two constituencies have different principles of emendation and address different audiences; but the improvement of the text, and the assumption that it required improvement, have been watchwords of both. About half of Shakespeare's plays have come down to us in multiple versions: the basic fluidity and malleability of Shakespeare's scripts is an essential fact about them, and that means there never was a final, correct text of any Shakespeare play. Revision was a part of the system; and though we tend to regard the two texts of *King Lear* as something like a first draft and a performing version, they are surely merely the only two of many versions of the play that have survived from Shakespeare's time.

Tate's version revises in ways we easily understand, even if we do not like them, clarifying, supplying motivations, justifying action, generally neatening and redirecting the play, particularly through an added romantic plot: Cordelia and Edgar are lovers. In Tate, Cordelia's rudeness at the opening is strategic, designed to prevent her father from marrying her off. In this way, motivations that are obscure in Shakespeare are supplied with a focus. The folio text itself is a revision, but it seems not to be Tate's sort of revision. Things one would think any reviser would want to clarify or edit out go unchanged. It is useful, therefore, to start with the folio's alterations to the quarto. What, to the earliest editors, was unsatisfactory about the play, and what constituted fixing it?

Some things in the quarto seem like false starts, afterthoughts, unreconciled changes of mind, or just plain muddles. At the beginning of Act 1 scene 5 Kent is sent with "letters" "to Gloucester": "Go you before to Gloucester with these letters." These turn out in the next clause, however, to be a single letter addressed not to Gloucester but to Regan: "Acquaint my daughter no further with anything you know than comes from her demand out of the letter." Editors (myself included) are reduced to explaining that Regan's castle must therefore be in the *city* of Gloucester, which has not been mentioned before and is never mentioned again. This strikes me as a dubious explanation, despite my complicity in it—Gloucester in the play never means anything except the Earl of Gloucester. It seems to me much more likely that Shakespeare's first idea was to have Lear send a packet of aggrieved letters to the Earl of Gloucester, including one for him to deliver to Regan, and then changed his mind without changing the line. In any case, if the topographical explanation is correct, it is a point that is impossible to convey in anything but a footnote: on stage, the reference to Gloucester is a red herring.

The puzzles in *Lear* continue: in Act 2 scene 1, the letter has been delivered by Kent and has prompted Regan and Cornwall to leave their castle and go to Gloucester's—we do not see the letter being delivered, but Kent has followed them, and in the next scene Regan and Cornwall recognize him as Lear's messenger. The puzzling scene with Kent berating Oswald follows, in which, when Cornwall questions the two, Kent refuses to defend himself, allows Oswald to give all the explanations, and is deliberately, pointlessly, rude to Cornwall. Left to spend the night in the stocks, Kent then produces a letter from Cordelia, "Who hath most fortunately been informed/Of my obscurèd course." This is the only indication of a continuing communication between Kent and Cordelia, which is obviously quite essential to the plot.

The folio revision clarifies none of this. The only significant change to these scenes is in Gloucester's protest against putting Kent in the stocks. In the quarto, Gloucester says, "His fault is much, and the good king his master/Will check him for't," and there follows a direct criticism of Cornwall:

Your purposed low correction
Is such as basest and contemned'st wretches
For pilf'rings and most common trespasses
Are punished with.[1] (1608: II.2.139–142)

That is, you don't do this to a gentleman. In the folio, both the assurance of a royal punishment and the reproach are removed, and the only sanction that remains from the quarto is the danger of angering the king:

The king his master needs must take it ill
That he, so slightly valued in his messenger,
Should have him thus restrained. (1623: II.2.141–143)

The changes make Gloucester both less naïve and more cautious in his treatment of Cornwall—this seems, like many of the folio's revisions, designed to effect a minor adjustment in character.[2] Why were the plot muddles left alone? A nicely postmodern line might be that they were considered desirable, even essential, so that the play resisted elucidation, a "dark conceit," as Spenser says *The Faerie Queene* is. I like the muddles, and the sense they give that more is going on in the action than the play reveals; but as an explanation, this again strikes me as unlikely: when Shakespeare wants to be obscure he is quite straightforward about it, as in *The Phoenix and the Turtle* and many passages in *Macbeth*, *Cymbeline*, and *The Winter's Tale*. It seems to me more likely that the process of revision was simply unsystematic, piecemeal, and occasional— the muddles, then as now, go by so quickly on stage that they pose problems mainly for editors and readers. Those problems were not what the actor-revisers (who may or may not have included Shakespeare) were concerned with. There is a good deal in the texts of most plays of the period that even the original audience must have missed.

The revisers do seem to have been concerned with pacing, which probably explains the cutting of Lear's mock-trial of Goneril and Regan in Act 3 scene 6, a favorite episode of modern directors. It is usually returned to the script now (modern productions are also usually too long). It *is* a good bit, but it holds up the action; and for plays that had to be performed in two or two and a half hours, it must have seemed expendable—what would you cut? For us, the answer would be as much of the fool as possible: his jokes are now unfunny, and their point is often unrecoverable. But he was precisely what would not have been cut in 1623; indeed, the folio's principal addition to the quarto is the fool's fifteen-line prophecy at the end of Act 3 scene 2, epigrammatically predicting a future identical to the present, about half of which now requires glosses to make sense. If such moments work at all for us, it is not through the text but through the actor's body language. For us, the fool is a marginal figure who gives a performance largely independent of the script.

The fool in Shakespeare's theater, however, was not marginal, but essential, the figure in whom the whole idea of performance itself was embodied, and the fact that his role was often unscripted only emphasizes the extent to which early modern drama was as much performative as textual. There is a delightfully indicative stage direction in an anonymous play called *The Tryall of Chevalrie* (1605) that reads, "Exit clown, speaking anything."[3] *King Lear* is the Shakespeare play in which the fool is most deeply germane to the action, Lear's zany conscience, Cordelia's antic alter ego. Why do we still keep the fool at all? He cannot simply be cut without radically altering the play (as Tate did, and duly cut the fool); but he could be made wise and witty, or at least funny, again—this is a case where sticking to the text really does violate the spirit of the role, which has always been improvisation. Suppose you cast an actor like Zero Mostel or Amy Schumer in the role, with instructions to do whatever he or she wanted. The fool's speeches are scripted, but it is not clear that they always were, and if Robert Armin, the principal clown of The King's Men, was the original fool, he would surely have been significantly involved in the development of the role.

The folio text is still much too long to have been a performing version, but it gives a sense of how the performers worked, what sorts of things could go, and what needed to be expanded—not, on the whole, the things we cut, and certainly not those we expand (for example, on the one hand, pageantry, and on the other, things that clarify the plot). There is one entirely logical revision in the folio text (in contrast to what we might call all the folio's performance-based revisions), the omission from the folio of Act 4 scene 3, with Kent's account of Lear being too ashamed to see Cordelia; this is an editorial revision. The scene is obviously part of an earlier idea about the play; there is no sign that Lear has been avoiding Cordelia when he finally does see her in Act 4 scene 7, and indeed, no indication that he knows she is in England at all: the two scenes contradict each other. This sort of editorial logic is very rare in the folio's alterations.

But now consider an illogical revision: only the quarto, in Act 5 scene 3, includes Edgar's account to Albany of meeting the disguised Kent just after the death of Gloucester and of Kent revealing himself (1608: V.3.204–218). Why would the folio cut this? Without it, Kent is never identified to Albany as Lear's mysterious retainer Caius, so that when Kent appears in the folio's play ten lines later, the only enlightenment Albany gets is Edgar's "Here comes Kent" (1623: V.3.205). Kent, as far as Albany knows, has been missing since the first scene and has had nothing to do with the subsequent action, and nothing explains his presence in the final scene. The folio produces a loose end that seems to have been deliberately untied. In fact, Kent never gets any kind of dramatic recognition at the end, in either version: he has come for a grand reconciliation with Lear, but he has to point out what everyone else has forgotten, that Lear is not even present. Lear himself never makes the connection between Kent and Caius. This was doubtless retained in the folio because it adds significantly to the pathos and abjectness of Lear's condition, but why then deliberately change the text to keep Albany in the dark too? Surely the irony and pathos are strongest if everyone knows Kent's double identity except Lear.

One might say that Albany does not need to know it; it is sufficient for the audience to know it, and it contributes to a kind of terminal vagueness. In contrast, however, the play also concludes with some compulsive tidying up: instead of relying simply on dramatic action, incriminating documents are produced, things that prove Goneril's villainy and Edmund's treachery, as if these were in question. For whom does evidence have to be produced? To whom is Edgar's chivalric victory and Edmund's confession insufficient to justify the treatment of the villains? Moreover, the evidence is just the kind Edmund had initially used to impeach Edgar with—why is a letter purporting to be from Goneril any more trustworthy than a letter purporting to be from Edgar? Letters delivered by villains are inherently problematic; that is, it is not the document but the moral status of its bearer that constitutes the proof (so much for documentary evidence!). But why is a letter necessary at all? Clearly in this case it is not enough for the audience to see the justice of Edgar's charges: Albany on stage must see it. But then why remove the lines that explain Kent's presence to Albany? The compulsive elucidation leaves lots of holes in the plot, even more in the folio text than in the quarto.

Revising, for modern writers, is a process of tidying up, but gaps and obscurities are not the things the folio's revisers wanted to deal with. In fact, the only significant thing in the plot that was altered is the removal of references to the French king and his army from Cordelia's reappearance to rescue her father. In Act 3 scene 1, the quarto says

> From France there comes a power
> Into this scattered kingdom, (1608: III.1.22–26)

which is revised to say merely that Albany and Cornwall have spies for the French among their servants. Similarly, Gloucester tells Edmund in the quarto that "there's part of a power already landed" to avenge the king (3.3.12–13), whereas in the folio the power is "already footed": the quarto's army comes from abroad, the folio's is domestic. But even this is not consistent: in Act 3 scene 7 lines 2–3 in both texts read, "The army of France is landed," though only the quarto has Kent and a gentleman in a later scene discussing details of the French military arrangements, with the king returning to France (1608: IV.3a.4). The change is generally explained as involving a political issue, but why should a French army on English soil be less politically sensitive in 1608 than later? In any case, Cordelia's presence must certainly constitute a French invasion; the folio merely softens the blow by removing the reference to the French king, so that the French troops become Cordelia's. The revision, however, also seems to make her abandon France to take charge of her father—her husband is effectively removed. In the folio, then, ironically, Cordelia does exactly what in the opening scene she swears she will never do, "marry like my sisters/To love my father all" (1.1.103–104). But maybe this is the point; maybe the folio wants Cordelia's reappearance to be sentimental rather than military.

Now consider a scene that neither the folio nor Tate cut, and that until well into the nineteenth century was both widely deplored and considered indispensable, the blinding of Gloucester. Johnson wrote of this "that the cruelty of the daughters is an historical fact . . . But I am not able to apologise with equal plausibility for the extrusion of Gloucester's eyes, which seems an act too horrid to be endured in dramatick exhibition, and such as must always compel the mind to relieve its distress by incredulity."[4] But Johnson continues with a strikingly relativistic apology for the scene: "Yet let it be remembered that our authour well knew what would please the audience for which he wrote." This begs some questions (the scene was still being played for the audiences of Johnson's time, and for decades thereafter) but Johnson's strategy here, to focus not on the stage, but on the audience, and on the audience, moreover, as an impediment to revision, is one I wish to pursue.

The blinding scene is in its way unique not only in Shakespearean drama but in the drama of the period. Hypocritical speeches, forged letters, sending elderly fathers out in the rain, not having respect for kingship, and conning one's brother out of his inheritance are all fairly unsurprising indices to villainy in Renaissance drama. How much more villainous do the villains have to be in *King Lear*? The villains' badness is literalized through torture and mutilation; but though the play often works by actualizing its metaphors—Lear's rage becoming the storm, Gloucester describing Regan's cruelty as plucking out Lear's eyes—one of the reasons the scene is so shocking is precisely the fact of how unprepared we are for it.

The scene's dramatic intensity is so powerful that it prompts a critical tendency to dissipate it, for example, by allegorizing it (it realizes Gloucester's moral blindness), and in fact the play does some of that as well: Gloucester himself later says "I have no way and therefore want no eyes/I stumbled when I saw" (4.1.18–19), and his response to the terrible taunt "Out vile jelly/Where is thy lustre now?" is "All dark and comfortless" (3.7.84–85), which is really impossible to say in a realistic performance—instead of a howl of pain, the actor is required to produce a brief, elegiac parallel with the comfortless Lear in the storm. In the theater, however, we are confronted not with textual parallels but with violent and painful action presented directly on stage. Giorgio Strehler's 1972 production turned the scene into a very kinky sexual game between Cornwall and Regan in black leather, with Gloucester invisible in the trap beneath. This has a point, in the sense that the scene is really establishing something about Cornwall and Regan, not about Gloucester—we know all the ways in which Gloucester is blind; what we do not know is the full force of evil realizing itself in the play. But real evil produces real blindness, and that might be a reason for keeping Gloucester onstage, forcing the scene on our eyesight.

Still, this does not quite describe what occurs dramatically, because after all, nothing really happens to Gloucester: this is a play. But if we withdraw from the scene in this way—Gloucester is a fictional character impersonated by various actors over and over, none of whom ever gets blinded—we are all the more aware that what happens in the scene happens not to the character but to the audience; and if we consider the scene in this light, it is not at all unique: there are many other comparable scenes. Elizabethan pamphlets are full of explicit accounts of horrible tortures inflicted on prisoners; and executions, sometimes involving drawing and quartering or burning alive, were a species of popular entertainment. John Foxe's book of martyrs *Actes and Monuments*, with its ghastly accounts of the sufferings of Protestant heroes, adorned with ghastly woodcuts, was a continual best seller throughout the age, not only for its devotional matter; the devotional and the lurid are clearly aspects of each other. It may be that tastes have changed somewhat in this respect, though they certainly have not changed so much that we cannot see the point—S&M is, after all, still very much in fashion, and sadism is increasingly a staple of popular movies. Maybe the point of this scene is just the opposite of the one we try to get out of it: we are horrified at the treatment of the good people by the bad people, outraged by the villainy of the villainous, but suddenly here is a scene that puts us firmly in collusion with the villains—this is the scene that gives Shakespeare's audience what they really like, the pleasures of torture and mutilation with a good moral context to boot. "Let it be remembered," says the judicious Johnson, "that our authour well knew what would please the audience for which he wrote."

So how bad are Cornwall and Regan? Just about as bad as we are; they are doing it for our pleasure. The folio makes one revision to the scene, deleting the pitying and moralizing servants. That seems designed to emphasize our complicity, to keep us focused on the theater of cruelty, to avoid introducing a surrogate pity that detaches us from the action. The scene, moreover, cannot be accounted for as an indication of the savagery of early modern taste: although commentators have been universally appalled by it, few revisers, and none till the mid-nineteenth century, found a way of doing without it. Tate says he could not think of a way of cutting it and maintaining the plot. Whatever else it is, it has seemed both structurally essential and a necessary principle of explanation. Still, it is hard to see the resistance to moving the blinding itself offstage as anything but disingenuous. The scene is simply too powerful a piece of theater for the performing tradition to abandon it.

The first recorded performance of *King Lear* is the one cited on the 1608 quarto titlepage, at court before King James, on December 26, 1606. There is no other known performance in London or at court before the Restoration; the only other early record concerns a private performance given by a provincial company in a gentleman's house in Yorkshire, a group of Catholic players, who were indicted in 1610 for performing Catholic propaganda. The particular charge was that they had performed *King Lear*, *Pericles*, and a lost play about St. Christopher. They defended themselves by asserting that their scripts were the published quartos of the plays, which had been licensed and could not therefore be called subversive or seditious. This defense was inadequate in two respects: first, the licensing of books is a different matter from the licensing of theatrical performances. Audiences are large and unpredictable; their responses constitute much more of a civic danger than do the responses of the readers of printed plays. But second, and perhaps more to the point, the relation between the licensed text of a play and the staged script is quite simply imponderable. This is why the licensing of plays included a specific injunction that no more was allowed to be spoken than appeared in the script, a stipulation that was as essential as it was unenforceable—it was the presumed violation of this principle that was at issue here. The most significant part of this story for modern assumptions about early playtexts is the testimony that the first quartos of *King Lear* and *Pericles*, which are both, for us, hornets' nests of editorial problems, were the bases for perfectly usable theatrical scripts in the period.[5]

The paucity of the stage history of *King Lear* is odd for so widely cited a play, and presumably means that we have lost the records, not that there were no performances. It was republished in quarto in 1655, when the theaters were closed; so there was still a market for it, and when the theaters reopened in 1660, it was frequently performed, first in the folio version, and then, ubiquitously, in Tate's revision, to which I now turn.

The happy ending is the most notorious of Tate's changes to the plot, though in a way it is the least surprising. As I have indicated, in every other version of the Lear story, both in the chronicles and in an earlier play called *The True Chronicle History of King Leir*, Cordelia ultimately triumphs, Lear's throne is restored to him, he dies in peace, and she rules after him. She is subsequently deposed, imprisoned, and commits suicide, but that is part of another story; she has heirs, and both the continuity of Lear's line and the facts of early British history are assured. Historically, she was succeeded by Goneril's son, which is ironic; but Edgar, on whom Shakespeare bestows the kingdom, has no place in the line of succession at all, and is a fictional character anyway. To kill off Cordelia and give the kingdom to Edgar was both historically perverse and a significant defeat for any early audience's expectations. It is not even clear in Shakespeare why Edgar should be promoted to the throne at all, to say nothing of Kent, whom Albany designates as co-ruler with Edgar, though Kent declines the honor.

Of the characters left alive, Albany himself would seem to have the best claim to succeed Lear, being both his son-in-law and the victor in the battle for the kingdom; but instead he ends the play by dividing up the kingdom again, this time between two people who have no claim to it. Is there really nothing here for critical commentary to take account of? Shakespeare is not especially faithful to history elsewhere, but this is surely an extreme example, analogous to making Henry V lose the battle of Agincourt, and installing somebody—anybody—else as king. From Tate to Johnson, a standard element in the defense of the happy ending was that it was true. It was Shakespeare who had changed the ending, not Tate. For Shakespeare's original audiences, the ending of the play was a surprise.

The question of why (and how) Shakespeare changed the ending has not been a serious one for us. Tate's ending, we argue, trivializes the suffering, though the subtext of this argument is surely that if Shakespeare did it, it must be right. But there is nothing normative, even within Shakespeare's own work, that dictated the tragic ending. What he added to a very mixed plot was a degree of abjectness and cruelty unmatched in his drama since *Titus Andronicus*. It is precisely those elements that we do not take seriously; Johnson takes them seriously, when he says that "I was many years ago so shocked by Cordelia's death, that I know not whether I ever endured to read again the last scenes of the play till I undertook to revise them as an editor."[6] Surely it is worth asking what seemed to require an outcome at once so bleak and so unexpected in a dramaturgy that could produce tragicomedy like *Measure for Measure*, *Cymbeline*, *Pericles*, and *The Winter's Tale*, all plays whose sufferings are redeemed in a reversal of fortune that we might even call characteristically Shakespearean.

The answer to this question may well be biographical and therefore beyond the limits of our evidence. Nevertheless, it is worth recognizing as an issue and insisting that the ending is not one that is determined by the plot. This is a play in which Shakespeare goes out of his way to raise expectations only to (perhaps in order to) defeat them. Cordelia's aborted survival is not the only one. What about the recognition of Edgar by the blind Gloucester, which is reported in a single line as an afterthought in *King Lear*, but is the start of the episode in Sidney's *Arcadia* that was Shakespeare's source, the perspective from which the whole story is told by the reconciled father and son? In Shakespeare, on the contrary, it is precisely the revelation of Edgar's identity that kills Gloucester.

Perhaps, however, we judge the general tone of the play, its exceptional bleakness, by an anachronistic standard. For us, Lear starts out with an obvious display of temperament, which unleashes all the problems. Notice, however, that though it is Kent who initially objects to Lear's bad judgment, only the villains believe that it renders him unfit to rule. In fact, elsewhere he is referred to in the play not as blind, foolish, irascible, self-centered, mad, or incompetent (or as we would sum it up, senile) but as *kind*—Kent says, "the hard rein which both of them have borne/Against the old kind king." (1623: III.1.19–20). Lear on himself, "So kind a father!" (I.5.32), is presumably to be taken ironically, but what he later says, "Your old kind father, whose frank heart gave all" (1608: III.4.19–20; 1623: III.4.20), is, objectively, accurate. When Richard Burbage, Shakespeare's leading man, died in 1619, his elegy lists the roles that made him famous:

> young Hamlet, old Hieronymo [in *The Spanish Tragedy*]
> kind Lear, the grievèd Moor [Othello][7]

Kind Lear. All these examples insist on Lear's essential goodness. For a Jacobean audience, however, the largest point would surely be that even a bad king is still the king. This is no doubt why this play about a monarch destroyed by his heirs was considered an appropriate entertainment for King James's court. For us, Shakespeare's play is about the responsibilities of kingship, how thoughtless small acts can have incalculably terrible effects, how little we understand even the people who are closest to us and, above all, about our capacity for suffering and about the fact that however bad things are, they can always be worse. But Shakespeare's surprise ending also impressed on Jacobean audiences that ignoring the patriarchal imperatives not only brought chaos to the kingdom but destroyed the line of succession, and indeed, overturned history itself. So perhaps our objections to the sentimentalization of the play that Tate's version represents are anachronistic. It was already quite a sentimental play; we have adopted the point of view of the villains. Tate's version is sentimental in a different way, but he does understand something about the play in Shakespeare's time that we have forgotten.

Many of Tate's revisions were dictated by contemporary political issues, but there are other considerations as well. There was the necessity for increasing the scope of the female roles for a theater in which women were now significant players. The basic question, however, is not what happens when women are played by women rather than by young men, but what differences the culture assumes between men and women, and what constitutes an acceptable representation of either. The issue here obviously has to do not with sex but with gender—not with chromosomes and genital organs but with codes of behavior.

In one respect, all the trouble is caused by Cordelia's initial refusal to give a performance. But good women in Shakespeare's society are *supposed* to be silent. Cordelia starts by playing the traditional female role, one that women are praised for, and that women in Shakespeare generally do not play. It is Lear who violates the traditional gender codes by forcing his daughters, especially the unmarried one, to speak. It is important to emphasize, however, that in this case the cultural norm is never a Shakespearean norm: think of Shakespeare's heroines Portia, Rosalind, Beatrice, Juliet. A counter-example such as the silent Virgilia in *Coriolanus* (her husband refers to her as "my gracious silence") is balanced in *Coriolanus* by Coriolanus's mother, the voluble Volumnia. In general, however, the issue of female volubility in Shakespeare is more conventional than gendered: in comedy, the female speakers are unmarried and good fun; in tragedy, they are married and disruptive, or even absolutely villainous: the murderous bullying of Lady Macbeth is reprehensible, but so, in *The Winter's Tale*, is the shrewish Paulina's entirely virtuous refusal to obey her husband and the king and be silent. As a cultural assumption, for wives to talk is much more dangerous than for unmarried women to do so: women eventually pass from their fathers' control but not from their husbands'. It must be to the point that the fathers of Portia, Viola, Olivia, Beatrice, Helena, and Isabella are all dead; and Rosalind's father, though alive, is effectively silenced and is given no say in his daughter's marriage arrangements.

The gender imperatives in *King Lear* actually seem less significant than the patriarchal imperatives; nor are these uniform: the patriarchy of fathers often conflicts with that of husbands. In fact, the position of husbands and fathers in the play is arguably more to the point than the position of women; husbands and fathers are the endangered species. Questions of inheritance, the basic patriarchal questions, are the key ones: Lear dividing his property in three is following Elizabethan law, by which, while sons inherit according to primogeniture (the eldest gets everything), daughters inherit equally. Legally, Lear's division of the kingdom is at fault only in attempting to give Cordelia a better share than her sisters. The problems of primogeniture are the subject of the Gloucester plot, where Edmund is doubly disadvantaged: he is not only illegitimate, he is the younger son as well. Even if he were legitimate he still would be entitled to nothing. The issue in all these cases has to do not with the position of sons as opposed to daughters but with the position of children in relation to their fathers and to each other.

What then does gender have to do with it? It is the focus of the erotics of the play, certainly, though these also have little to do with the issues of marriage that fill the opening scene—"tell me how much you love me" is what fathers say to children in *King Lear*, not what lovers say to each other. As for the erotics of the opening scene, Burgundy and France have come to woo Cordelia, but for both, the primary issue is inheritance, not love. There is absolutely nothing culturally inappropriate about this: the reason women in this culture are provided with dowries is that men will not marry them otherwise. Women are property, and the more property they represent the more desirable they are.

So why does Cordelia become more attractive to the king of France when she is dowryless and out of favor with the king? This is the romance element in the plot; the love interest suddenly materializes and is represented as entirely quixotic. Of course, France's romantic passion can also be seen realistically (or cynically) as representing basically an investment. France supporting an invasion of England by an army led by his wife is hardly disinterested; France is not concerned solely to get Lear in out of the rain. To rescue Lear is to repossess Cordelia's third of the kingdom, and perhaps much more. Cordelia is a gamble, but in all the sources the gamble pays off handsomely—Cordelia becomes queen. The surprise for a Jacobean audience would have been that in Shakespeare it does not pay off.

Where then are the erotics of the play? They are in the villains, the adulterous passion of Goneril and Regan for Edmund, which turns the sisters from natural allies to natural enemies. In Shakespeare's version, this has much more to do with plotting and villainy than with passion: we hear about the sisters' pursuit of Edmund, and Edmund admits that he has courted both, but there are no love scenes. Edmund is sometimes played as glamorous and sexually magnetic; that works very well, but it really is adding a dimension to the play that is scarcely suggested. The love affairs in the text are all basically just more intrigue: the lust on Edmund's side is for power; and as for the sisters, so far as we can tell, they kill each other off before any sex happens. Gloucester's past adultery casts an increasingly ominous shadow, but is there any evidence of adultery taking place in the play's present tense? The lust and passion consist, dramatically at least, of writing letters, which ultimately get revealed to the one surviving husband. The adultery is literally textual.

Tate's most significant alteration to Shakespeare's plot comes not at the
end but at the beginning: Cordelia and Edgar are in love. This is Tate's way
of accounting for Cordelia's behavior in the opening scene: her refusal to play
Lear's game is strategic, preventing her from being married off to Burgundy
(France has been entirely eliminated). As a dramatic device, the romance has
come under attack since the eighteenth century; and it does certainly neaten
and rationalize the plot. But in fact Cordelia's behavior in the opening scene
has always been a problem—is she culpable or not? In their reconciliation
scene in Act 4, when Lear tries to apologize, her response is "No cause, no
cause" (1608: IV.6.74; 1623: 72): if that is not simply empty politeness, it constitutes an apology of her own, acknowledging that she is in some sense culpable, that the issue at the outset was not simply honest silence versus lying
rhetoric, but involved both a violation of courtesy and an insensitivity to the
infirmity of her father's condition and the complexity of his nature. After all,
what is on trial in the opening scene is not only Cordelia's love for Lear, but
more deeply, Lear's love for Cordelia—she knows he loves her best. If Lear
throws away Cordelia's love, so does Cordelia throw away Lear's. One may not
want this issue settled, or sidestepped, so neatly, but criticism has on the whole
idealized Cordelia in this scene, and Tate confronts a question that commentators have preferred to avoid.

If love is a principle of explanation in Tate's *King Lear*, lust is a principle
of politics—Tate brings into the open things that are implied or alluded to
in Shakespeare but seem to be underplayed; and in the Restoration revision a
careful balance of the erotic and the political is maintained. The most spectacular scene in Tate's revision is the attempted rape of Cordelia by Edmund: sex
is a destructive weapon, a way of getting revenge and exerting control. (She is
rescued, of course, by Edgar.) Tate's Edmund begins his ascent by announcing
his passion for "the proud imperial sisters."[8] Gloucester's rebellious support of
Lear is explicit and forceful: Cordelia, who is present throughout the action,
enlists his aid, and he replies that "I have already plotted to restore/My injured
master" (23–24). They are overheard by Edmund, who declares his passion for
Cordelia and his intention of betraying his father in the same speech. He says
he will kidnap Cordelia and then rape her as the wind and thunder drown
out her cries. The attack on Cordelia and her rescue by Edgar was one of the

great set pieces of Tate's play. The scene concludes with Cordelia and Edgar declaring and confirming their love.

The blinding scene follows this. Tate speeds it up and lingers less than Shakespeare over the sadism. He also, characteristically, adds an erotic twist: as Edmund is sent away in deference to his filial feelings, he is propositioned by Regan and goes off to await her in a grotto. The blinded Gloucester, thrust out of doors, determines to remain a political force:

> I will present me to the pitying crowd,
> And with the rhetoric of these dropping veins
> Enflame 'em to revenge their king and me. (33)

Exactly what Goneril and Regan fear in Shakespeare comes to pass in Tate. Regan and Edmund's love scene in the grotto immediately follows.

The Dover Cliff scene is retained, but Tate frames it with scenes of the growing rebellion. The revived Gloucester persuades Kent to lead the troops, and a Cordelia who by this time has little in common with Shakespeare's heroine ends Act 4 with a warlike speech. After this the play moves to its conclusion with a mass of plotting. Goneril orders poison to be prepared for Regan; Edmund plans a move from Regan, with whom he has already slept, to Goneril, whom he has yet to possess:

> Cornwall is dead, and Regan's empty bed
> Seems cast by fortune for me, but already
> I have enjoyed her, and bright Goneril
> With equal charms brings dear variety,
> And yet untasted beauty (46)

Tate's Edmund speaks with the erotic sensibility of a Restoration rake, but the underlying sexual politics are Shakespeare's.

At the end, where Shakespeare's Albany gives the kingdom to Kent and Edgar, Tate's Albany gives it to Cordelia and Edgar. The marriage Tate invents for them in one sense subverts Shakespeare's conclusion, but in another sense vindicates it: the only way for Edgar to succeed to the throne is as Cordelia's husband. Tate's *King Lear* is sentimental and melodramatic; it is also clear, well paced, dramatically effective, and as its long presence in the theater confirms, eminently stageable. From a modern perspective, it is most interesting as a critical reading of Shakespeare, confronting genuine problems in the play. We have, on the whole, preferred to deal with these through elucidation and commentary, rather than through theatrical revision—we tend now to prefer bibliographical explanations (and revisions) to narrative ones; but what that does is move the play increasingly away from the stage and toward the book and the putative manuscript behind it.

—(2005)

10

Venice at the Globe

Elizabethan England viewed Venice as a model of an equitable society. William Thomas's *Historie of Italie,* published in 1549 under Edward VI, holds up Venice as a pattern for good government, not least in the ways it resembles England, with its impartial legal system and its Great Council as a parallel to Parliament. Thomas's optimistic view of the fairness of the English system was not borne out under Mary Tudor, when he was implicated in Thomas Wyatt's rebellion and executed for sedition. But especially in the later years of Elizabeth's reign, when the succession remained unsettled and aristocratic republican ways of determining the future seemed increasingly attractive, the Venetian model as described by Thomas was often invoked for comparison. There is no evidence that Shakespeare had read Thomas's *Historie,* though he would certainly have known about it; but by the time he was writing *The Merchant of Venice* he may have read Lewes Lewkenor's *Commonwealth and Government of Venice* in manuscript—the book was published in 1599, but it was a translation of a 1549 Latin treatise by Gasparo Contarini. The influence of these works on Elizabethan and Jacobean England has been widely appreciated and well treated elsewhere.[1]

Here I am concerned not with historical sources but with the way Venice is imagined for the English stage. Judging from the drama, if Venice is seen as a model for England, it is a very ambiguous one; and as a mirror, it primarily reflects England's fears and vices. For example, Portia's confounding of

Shylock and rescue of Antonio is a dramatic climax in *The Merchant of Venice*, a triumph of both romantic ingenuity and legal strategy; but neither Portia's methods nor her arguments would have passed muster in an Elizabethan court (to say nothing of a Venetian one), and later audiences have generally found the scene more disturbing than celebratory.

The Venice of Antonio and Shylock is a burgeoning early capitalist economy, a world of merchants, importers and exporters, investors, and those largely invisible but nevertheless essential figures who make the whole system work, the suppliers of risk capital, particularly moneylenders. Antonio's money comes from trade, Shylock's from what the Elizabethans pejoratively called usury and we would call simply banking. Neither can prosper without the other, and the system requires both. Antonio claims there are moneylenders in Venice who charge no interest, but clearly none of them will deal with him: given his investment in Bassanio, he is obviously a bad risk. Shylock takes the risk—he is essential, both to the plot and to Antonio's and Bassanio's enterprise. His decision not to charge interest in this case is intended only as a way of ensuring future business from Antonio, another kind of investment. The people in this society who are not dependent on the system, who do not make their money but simply have it—the rich heiresses—live somewhere else. Significantly, the somewhere is a geographical fantasy, Belmont: the name is adopted from the source story in *Il Pecorone,* and it is the only invented place name in Shakespeare.

Ben Jonson's Venetian play *Volpone* is about a clever scoundrel who fleeces his equally unsavory associates by pretending he is dying and persuading them that he will make one of them his heir. They each give him increasingly rich gifts in the hope of being confirmed as the favorite. Though the names—Volpone, Mosca, Corvino, Corbaccio—suggest a moralizing beast-fable, this Venice is a thoroughly capitalistic world, full of merchants, investors, lawyers, and notaries. Corbaccio, the "big crow," who disinherits his son in favor of Volpone, is a miser—in a capitalist economy, that is tantamount to being a thief. Only Corbaccio's son, the soldier Bonario, and Celia, the merchant Corvino's wife, are declared by their names to be human, humane, and virtuous in a world that allows them very little space. Even the miser is in his way an investor, risking his money (and his son) in the interests of a significant return. Venice in the play is

an object of envy to two English travelers: its obsessions are parodied by Sir Politic Would-Be, who arrives full of impossibly grandiose moneymaking projects,
and his wife, Lady Would-be, who is as grasping and flirtatious as any Venetian
courtesan. The only disinterested voice is that of the one other English traveler,
Peregrine, who stands outside the action as an amused observer of his compatri-
ots' follies in pursuit of Italian vices—in effect, his voice is Jonson's.

The play opens with Volpone worshipping at the shrine of his gold. But
where does Volpone's money come from? Jonson is quite explicit: his wealth
does not derive from the mercantile economy in any way:

> *Vol.*   I gain
> No common way; I use no trade, no venture;
> I wound no earth with plough-shares;
> . . . have no mills for iron,
> Oil, corn; or men to grind them into powder: . . .
> I turn no monies in the public bank,
> Nor usure private[2]

and much more of the same sort of thing. As far as capitalism is concerned,
Volpone is not involved. Why the insistence on this, with such specificity?
When Stefan Zweig did his beautiful adaptation of the play in 1926,[3] he added
a prologue to account both for where Volpone's money came from (imports
and exports; one of his ships has just returned laden with riches) and for how
he and Mosca know each other (they met in jail, while Volpone was briefly
imprisoned for debt). These are matters which Jonson leaves significantly
unexplained. Zweig's version humanizes, rationalizes, and simplifies: it is an
easier, nicer play. But Jonson's Volpone is not merely a very successful merchant. He does not make money, he gets people to give it to him. To produce
money in the way Volpone boasts of doing, you have to start with money. The
play insists, however, that Volpone's hands are clean; his money is the product
of his wit, his ingenious scheming—as Iago says of Roderigo in another Venice, "Thus do I ever make my fool my purse."[4]

It cannot be irrelevant that the witty devising of plots is the source of the
playwright Jonson's income too. Volpone the master-manipulator is the heart

of this comedy and the source of our pleasure in it. As an appreciative audience, we are just as surely implicated in his schemes as Jonson is; and in the dramatic economy, here as in Jonson's even more popular play *The Alchemist*, no sympathy at all is elicited by the victims, who are by turns gullible and rapacious, and are represented as deserving what they get. The exceptions in *Volpone* are Celia and Bonario, but they serve more as foils than as agents. Bonario, the honest soldier, the man of action, is singularly ineffective; and all the play can offer Celia as a reward for her patience and virtue is to be sent home to her father with her dowry tripled, presumably only to find an even more covetous husband.

Volpone is all about money and about using money to make more. Jonson's fox is a scoundrel, but he is surely as much hero as villain—indeed, it is not clear that he is a villain at all. He is thoroughly amoral, certainly, but there is no suggestion that the gold he worships at the play's opening is ill-gotten. Indeed, as we have seen, it is explicitly denied that he has even been touched by the necessary evils of trade. Nor has he anything against his victims, no scores to settle, no revenge to exact: he cons them for the pure pleasure of the game; he lays out the bait, and they take it willingly, eagerly. The bait is the promise of an inheritance, of being Volpone's heir, being the surrogate son, brother, widow, the best beloved. In Jonson's Venice, affection and family ties have a cash value; Corvino is willing to prostitute his wife to Volpone; Corbaccio to disinherit his son; Lady Politic Would-Be abandons her husband for Volpone. The purpose of these outrageous acts is precisely to prompt a reciprocal act of what in this society counts as love.

This is a world in which love is money. We could call it particularly Jonsonian because it is particularly blatant; but it is in fact no different from the Venice of Shakespeare's merchants and lovers. At the opening of *The Merchant of Venice*, the first thing Bassanio says about Portia is that she is "a lady richly left" and will be the means of getting him out of debt (1.2.161). Romance is doubtless an element, but the money is essential: however beautiful, witty, or charming Portia is, she is nothing to Bassanio, or to any of her other suitors, without her money. She is, moreover, curiously like Volpone, in that she is in no way implicated in the acquisition of her wealth—this is obviously a fundamental element in her attractiveness. She does not *make* her money, she *has* her money. Moreover, her father's will stipulates that for a suitor to fail in choosing the correct casket requires forswearing marriage entirely. This practically ensures that only desperate fortune-hunters will come to woo her: who else would take so great a risk; why else would Bassanio do it? There is a great deal of talk about love in the play, but money is always a part of it. When Jessica elopes with her lover Lorenzo, she comes to him with a box of Shylock's gold, and later Shylock is observed alternately lamenting his daughter and his ducats, unable to decide which loss he regrets more. Surely in this world, the two are not separable: daughters *are* ducats. Lorenzo does not woo Jessica in the expectation of being poor but happy, any more than Bassanio considers proposing to Portia that they forget about the caskets and just run away together.

Daughters are ducats not only in drama but in the England of Shakespeare and Jonson too. Women are provided with dowries in early modern society because no one will marry them otherwise; daughters are their fathers' property, and, provided they are furnished with sufficient wealth, they can be exchanged for alliances, influence, property, position. That is why elopement is so highly charged an issue in the early modern world: children are commodities; they do not own themselves. Elopement is a form of theft. *Othello* and *Romeo and Juliet* would have looked quite different to Elizabethan and Jacobean audiences from the way they look to us. As I have observed in the essay "Two Household Friends," *Romeo and Juliet* is about a thirteen-year-old girl eloping with a fifteen-year-old boy: the parents in Shakespeare's audience would certainly have found the romance of the play tempered by some quite realistic apprehension. For us, a historically authentic production would probably bring charges of pedophilia.

As for the elopement of Desdemona and Othello, the degree to which it must have been disturbing to Shakespeare's audiences can be measured by the play's efforts to account for and justify it. Though Brabantio denies that he ever had any intention of making Othello his son-in-law, Desdemona's love for the Moor is clearly an extension of her father's, as Othello makes clear: "Her father loved me, oft invited me" (1.3.128ff.). Othello, moreover, is presented as genuinely irresistible: even the Duke says of his account of the wooing, "I think this tale would win my daughter too" (1.3.171). What is irresistible is his narrative, his command of language and plot; and just as Volpone's power is Jonson's power, Othello's power is Shakespeare's.

But Shakespeare's power is also Iago's, the ability to invent plots and stage scenes, and especially the ability to create entirely plausible fictions. Nor do we know that Iago is the play's only liar: Othello's narratives are beautifully crafted, but are they true? Consider the handkerchief: in the course of the play, he tells two entirely different stories about it. In the first, his mother had it from an Egyptian sorceress who wove it out of sacred silk dyed in mummy conserved of maidens' hearts (3.4.69–75); but in the second, much more mundanely, it was simply a gift his father gave his mother (5.2.216–217). Both stories cannot be true; is the invented one Othello's only lie? Audiences are necessarily trusting souls, and only the playwright can tell us what to believe—are the two handkerchief stories hints that we are being too trusting? Are the stories of Othello's heroic past, the exotic tales that Desdemona fell in love with, true or false? *We* know that the men whose heads do lie beneath their shoulders are fables, but did Shakespeare know it, and in that case, did Othello know it? Such questions really do get to the heart of the play: the corollary to the question of whether Othello is telling the truth is the much more highly charged question of whether Desdemona is really innocent. Not even Iago believes she is sleeping with Cassio, but maybe Iago's lies are true to some deep dubiousness in the play itself, some deep ambivalence on Shakespeare's part.

There really is some evidence for this, some significant loose ends. In Act 2, Othello tells Iago that Cassio was involved in his wooing of Desdemona from first to last; yet at the beginning of the play, when Iago tells Cassio that Othello is married, Cassio is surprised and claims not to know who his wife is. Is Cassio lying, and is the lie covering something up—is Othello's marriage to Desdemona really a surprise to Cassio? How could it be, if he was in on the wooing? What would make Othello's marriage unexpected? And in that case, might Iago's great lie, the lie on which the whole plot depends, in fact be the truth? Or shall we say that Shakespeare's plotting is always inconsistent, that he likes loose ends, as when Cassio is initially described as "A fellow almost damned in a fair wife" (1.1.20) but is thereafter unmarried. And do those inconsistencies then perhaps reveal something about Shakespeare's creative imagination: that any narrative contains within it a world of alternative narratives? Might Shakespeare be suspicious of Desdemona and Cassio, too?

Many years ago a deliberately provocative critic named Howard Felperin made a similar suggestion about *The Winter's Tale*: do we really know that Hermione is not guilty?[5] Her innocence is confirmed by an oracle, but for a Renaissance Christian audience, the deceptiveness of oracles was a given; to believe in them was to believe in a discredited faith. So at the Globe in 1610, the oracle might have actually seemed evidence confirming Leontes's suspicions. Felperin's suggestion was not intended to rewrite the play but to unsettle our notions of what we think we know in Shakespeare. After all, the entire resolution of *The Winter's Tale* depends on Leontes's willingness to believe in the miracle of a statue coming to life, a miracle that we know is a lie. Do satisfactory resolutions, then, depend on gullibility, whether the heroes' or the audience's? In *Othello*, we know Iago is not telling the truth, but we only know because he keeps admitting it: how do we assess the veracity of anyone else in the play? This is a continuing issue in *Hamlet*: is the Ghost telling the truth? Hamlet's doubts about the Ghost are both well founded and culturally justified: Protestant theology denied the existence of ghosts; apparitions were diabolical temptations. The only surprise for an Elizabethan audience might well have been that the Ghost turns out to be honest. Much of the action of the play involves setting up a test of the Ghost's story, the production of some credible evidence.

But evidence in Shakespeare is at many critical moments unreliable—telltale letters, for example, often turn out to be forged. Should we not expect some of Hamlet's skepticism in *King Lear*, from Gloucester, when presented with a threatening letter purporting to come from his son Edgar, or in *Twelfth Night* from Malvolio finding an extremely unlikely love letter from his mistress Olivia? Why, at the end of *Othello*, is there that litany of documentation, the notes found in Iago's handwriting, the letters found in Roderigo's pocket, that prove Iago's villainy? For whom by this time in the play is the issue in doubt? The answer can only be, for Shakespeare. But do the letters really prove anything? Suppose, like Olivia's love letter to Malvolio and Edgar's conspiratorial letter to Edmund, the notes found on Roderigo had been forged by Cassio—not an inconceivable plot twist, given the surprise endings of *King Lear* or *The Winter's Tale*. Suppose, without knowing it, Iago was on to something.

Audiences take a great deal on faith, and dramatic plotting, especially in comedy, depends heavily on gullibility. The brief scene in *The Merchant of Venice* in which the clown Launcelot Gobbo persuades his old, blind father that the son he has come to Venice to find is dead might be a touchstone for the play's dramatic strategy. Abstracted from its context, the situation is exceedingly painful. The fact that it is here a comic routine says much about the play as a whole. It is no news that sixteenth-century comedy included a good deal of cruelty, but the comedy here seems especially forced. The scene is over almost before it has begun; it is singularly pointless except as an index to family relations in the play's world. The old father is easy to deceive, being blind; the deception leaves him believing he is bereft of the person he cares most about. His situation is a grotesque version of both Shylock's and Antonio's, the only difference being that Gobbo's tragic loss is almost instantly reversable—and even then, Gobbo has difficulty believing that his son Launcelot is not only alive but has actually been the one playing this painful joke. But compare the moment in the trial scene when Portia and Nerissa hear their husbands declare that they would wish their wives dead if that would preserve Bassanio's beloved Antonio: this is presented as both a joke and a justification for Portia's ring trick. Marriage is always a dangerous business in Shakespeare, but it is rarely so openly a power game. There is surely something chillingly cold-blooded about Portia, more than a vestige of her original in *Il Pecorone*, in which the character is a widow who drugs her suitors and then robs them, and only accepts the Bassanio character on his third try.

Why are these plays set in Venice? Is Shakespeare's and Jonson's Venice even recognizably Venice? Shakespeare's source for *The Merchant* in *Il Pecorone* is set in Venice, which is reason enough for preserving the locale; but Antonio's and Shylock's Venice could easily be London. The only local color, the only place name in the play, is the Rialto, which Shakespeare thinks is the name of a bridge, rather than the name of the district in which the bridge is located. Shakespeare's Venice, moreover, has a significant Jewish population but no ghetto—the Venetian ghetto had been in existence since 1506. In what sense is this Venice?

Its connection with London is especially striking when we consider Shylock. Despite two centuries' of editorial attempts to identify Shylock as a biblical name, it is not Jewish, it is unambiguously English, and it had been an English surname since Saxon times. Shylock means "white-haired," like its more common cognates Whitlock and Whitehead, and has never had anything to do with Jews.[6] The other Jews in the play have obviously biblical names: Tubal, Cush, Leah. Critics have racked their brains over this; but Shylock is, like any number of Shakespeare's clowns and grotesques in exotic locales, ono-mastically English, and the continuing attempt to confine him in what is surely a critical ghetto reveals more about us than about Shakespeare. To be brief, there are many parallels to the English Shylock. The Navarre of *Love's Labour's Lost* includes Nathaniel and Costard (the most English of apples); all the Athe-nian workmen in *A Midsummer Night's Dream* have English names—Snout, Bottom, Snug, Quince, Flute, Starveling; the Mediterranean duchy of Illyria, roughly the modern Croatia, is home to the relentlessly English Sir Toby Belch and Sir Andrew Aguecheek; the servants in the Verona of *Romeo and Juliet* are Sampson, Gregory, Peter, and Abraham (and no critic to my knowledge has ever claimed that Sampson and Abraham must be Jews); the villain in the Sicily of *Much Ado About Nothing*, a world of Pedros, Leonatos, Claudios, and Bora-chios, is Don John. Shakespeare often wanted his clowns and grotesques to be recognizably English. Why is only Shylock's name a problem for us?

The moneylenders of Shakespeare's England, moreover, were not the Jews but anyone with some extra cash, including Shakespeare's father, who in 1570 was indicted for charging excessive interest on a loan, and William Shake-speare himself, who in 1609 was suing for repayment of a loan he had made to a Stratford man. The usury deplored by Antonio may be represented by Shakespeare as Italian, but Shylock's business is as English as his name. If I were hunting for the real Shylock of Shakespeare's imagination, I would look not in Old Testament genealogies but in the continuing Elizabethan debates on banking and interest—for example, in Thomas Wilson's *Discourse upon Usury* (1572) and more particularly in R. H. Tawney's masterful long intro-duction to the modern edition.[7] The Shylocks of Shakespeare's world were absolutely ubiquitous; by the end of the sixteenth century they began to be localized in a few groups: goldsmiths, mercers, and scriveners. None of these had anything to do with Jews; the association of Jews with usury in England was entirely conventional. Wilson, on the contrary, is convinced that the rise of usury was precisely a function of Protestantism, of Reformation morality and the abandonment of canon law. As Tawney says, "Calvin approached [economic life] as a man of affairs, who assumed, as the starting point of his social theory, capital, credit, large-scale enterprise,"[8] and therefore considered borrowing at interest essential. Much of Shylock's language recalls Puritan rhetoric. Shakespeare has little sympathy with Puritanism, but his distaste for it is not a distaste for outsiders.

If Antonio's and Shylock's Venice looks very much like London, Volpone's Venice might as well be the London of *The Alchemist.* In fact, one suspects that Jonson set the play in Venice not because of anything Italian but precisely to avoid London. Consider the date: the play was written very quickly early in 1606—Jonson says it took him six weeks. It was being performed at the Globe in the spring, so it would have been written at the latest in February and March, directly in the aftermath of the Gunpowder Plot; the trial of the plotters took place on January 27. Jonson was acquainted with the conspirators and had been present at at least one of their meetings. When the plot was revealed he was arrested and interrogated, and subsequently served as a government agent to prove his loyalty. Obviously he felt deeply threatened: he had already been in trouble with the law several times. He had killed an actor in a duel in 1598 and escaped hanging by pleading benefit of clergy (that is, by proving that he was literate); during his time in prison he converted to Catholicism. He again served prison time over passages deemed offensive to the court in the play *Eastward Ho,* of which he was a co-author; and in 1605 was called before the Privy Council on charges of sedition related to his play *Sejanus.*

Therefore in a new play produced in the spring of 1606, one would expect Jonson to tread carefully. So the play is set in Venice, but London is in the air. The cast, in addition to its menagerie of Italian animals, includes the three English travelers, Sir Politic Would-Be and his wife, who have been in Venice for some time, and Peregrine, who has recently arrived from London. Early in the play, Peregrine and Sir Politic meet in the Piazza San Marco, the only place name mentioned in the play. Sir Politic is eager for news from home; he has heard "a most strange thing reported" and wants details. The strange thing turns out not to be the Gunpowder Plot, the explosive news that is on everyone's lips both in the audience and throughout Europe, but that a raven has built a nest in one of the English royal ships. Peregrine doubts that Sir Politic can be serious and wonders whether he is being teased, but decides that his countryman really is the fool that he seems and duly produces a litany of trivia: a lion gave birth in the Tower of London; porpoises were seen near London Bridge; a whale was sighted at Woolwich; accounts of messages hidden by spies in toothpicks and pumpkins are reported; and much more of the same. It is clear that something is being avoided—Jonson's Venice is the London that dare not speak its name.[9]

As for the Venice of *Othello,* it is even less specific than the Venice of *The Merchant of Venice* and *Volpone.* Iago is sent to an inn called the Saggitary to fetch Desdemona. That is the only place name mentioned, and it appears to be Shakespeare's invention. The only element we could call realistic in *Othello*'s Venice is that the city is a melting pot, a world of outsiders. Cassio early in the play is identified as a Florentine—this is one of the things Iago holds against him; moreover, his given name, Michael, is English. Brabantio's name implies a Burgundian or Netherlandish origin; Iago and Roderigo are Spanish names; but the strangest name of all is Desdemona. This is the only name Shakespeare took from his source in Giraldi Cinthio's *Hecatommithi,* where she is the only named character, and the name appears in the form Disdemona. This invented name—it occurs nowhere else—may derive from the Greek Dis, the god of the Underworld, and daimon, spirit, so Hell-Spirit; or, less melodramatically, from the Greek dys-, bad, and daimon, so ill-fated (as Othello sums her up, "O ill-starred wench," 5.2.273). In either case, the implications of the name are more ominous than romantic, an embodiment of all Othello's worst fears.

Why, in a play that includes so many unproblematic Italian names (Emilia, Bianca, Gratiano, Lodovico, Montano) did Shakespeare import so many foreigners and retain Desdemona from his source? Are its ominous overtones perhaps part of the point; is Desdemona there as a warning of what is to come, the personification of the dangers of elopement and of Othello's love of danger? "She loved me for the dangers I had passed/ And I loved her that she did pity them" (1.3.171–172)—this circular love revolves around danger. As for the name Othello, it is Shakespeare's invention, a diminutive of Otho, and that may have some relevance: the historical Otho's wife, the notorious and dangerous Poppaea, cuckolded Otho with the Emperor Nero and eventually divorced him to marry the emperor. Otho was sent off to be governor of Lusitania. A decade later Otho briefly became emperor, succeeding Galba in a coup, but reigned only for three months. He was defeated in battle by the invading Vitellius and committed suicide as Othello does, by stabbing himself.

It is worth noting that Cinthio's story is not even set in Venice. It takes place entirely on Cyprus; we are only told that Disdemona's Venetian family had not wanted her to marry the Moorish captain. The play's Venice, then, relentlessly unspecific as it is, is all Shakespeare. As for Shakespeare's Cyprus, it is not clear when the play's action is imagined as taking place, but by 1606 Cyprus had for thirty-five years been a Turkish possession. Othello's victorious sea-battle, if it has any objective correlative at all, is an exercise in nostalgia.

Why are these plays set in Venice? It will be observed that there is nothing straightforward about any of these examples—London audiences are not simply being given a glimpse of a favorite stop on the Grand Tour; the plays are not travelogues. Quite the contrary: foreign places may be dangerous, but the dangers are home-grown. What Shakespeare and Jonson know about Venice is what they know about London.

—(2017)

11

Danny Scheie's Shakespeare

Danny Scheie made his debut as a professional director with an audacious and hilarious *Comedy of Errors* for Shakespeare Santa Cruz in 1988. Since then, and as artistic director of the company for four years in the 1990s, he has been responsible for a remarkable series of innovative Shakespeare productions, many performed outdoors, in a redwood grove on the campus of the University of California at Santa Cruz. His work, even at its most deliberately outrageous (at San Francisco's Theater Rhinoceros, for example, an all-male, frankly homoerotic *Twelfth Night* with Malvolio omitted), has seemed to me consistently interesting and genuinely enlightening about elements of the Shakespeare text that tend to be ignored or even suppressed by the editorial and critical tradition. The indignation his productions often evoke is a measure of how genuinely unsettling his readings tend to be for people devoted to settled notions of Shakespeare.

For the final play of his tenure at Shakespeare Santa Cruz in 1995, Scheie appropriately chose *The Tempest*. It was a brilliantly irreverent production, endlessly inventive, wildly funny, and even, on occasion, passionate and moving. Scheie's *Tempest* was undeniably not serious about any of the things the play is supposed to be serious about: magic, science, nature, art, Grace. Scheie also ignored the recent critical history of the play; his *Tempest* had as much to do with colonialism as does *Gilligan's Island*—to which, indeed, in one of many sight-gags, it alluded.[1] The production was certainly a send-up, though its target was less the play than traditional pieties about the play: the spirit of Charles Ludlam was very much in evidence. Some of the play's richness got lost in the excitement, but the excitement was real, and rare. Every production is a selective version of the text, and Scheie's *Tempest* remained deeply in touch with a dimension that most directors ignore or understate: its essential character as both spectacular theater and comedy. This is the drama in which Shakespeare makes the fullest use of the mechanical, visual, and auditory resources of his stage, employing flying machines, ascents, and descents, appearing and disappearing properties, storm effects, and more music than any other of his dramas. Scheie's *Tempest* was about the possibilities of comic theater.

And the play was unabashedly a comedy here, not a "romance." The single set was an absurdly steeply raked stage with three cloud curtains at the rear, liberally accommodated with trapdoors. The decor, insofar as there was a consistent one, suggested the 1950s: Miranda listened to the offstage shipwreck victims on a short-wave radio (the storm consisted of lawn sprinklers in the redwood grove, populated for the moment by Prospero's spirits, a group of screaming pre-adolescent girls in swimsuits), Prospero controlled Caliban with electrodes, the nymphs wore sci-fi outfits that recalled *Forbidden Planet*, Miranda viewed her past through a plastic stereopticon, and Prospero's magic book was *Popular Science*. But the production was contemporary enough when it wanted to be: Miranda was a Calvin Klein nymphet in minimalist cutoff jeans, Prospero revealed his intentions on a large color monitor, and the storm was played out to the musical theme from *The Poseidon Adventure*. The play was full of sight and sound gags: Ariel was summoned and directed with a television aerial, Alonso's banquet was a gigantic TV dinner with Ariel as the meat, the villains appeared on the television screen as the Wicked Witch of the West in *The Wizard of Oz*, the action was intermittently punctuated with the Blondie song *The Tide Is High*, bits of Bach cantatas abounded, and "Flout 'em and scout 'em" was sung to the music of "Sind Blitze, sind Donner, in Wolken verschwunden" from the *Saint Matthew Passion*, which fits it astonishingly well.

Irwin Appel's Prospero was radically unorthodox, with no trace of either Gielgud's benign magician or Michael Hordern's disaffected intellectual. A mad scientist in a black fright wig playing with a chemistry set, he had a zany comic intensity, delivering his lines as a combination of Zero Mostel and Wallace Shawn. Ariel, beautifully played by Eric Newton, was an elegant gymnast in silver tights, a creature of extraordinary lightness and charm who spent much of his time doing complicated things on a trapeze at the rear of the stage. Jack Zerbe's Caliban, in perhaps the most unorthodox of Scheie's realizations, was an eerily striking figure, not at all deformed, but classically muscular, naked except for his silver G-string and the electrodes that keep him in thrall to Prospero. His intense physical presence maintained a dignity even in the most anarchic of his scenes with Stephano and Trinculo. In most productions the play's drunken comedy tends to be embarrassing or tiresome; here it was beautifully controlled and genuinely funny. I have never seen these scenes more convincingly done. Susannah Schulman's Miranda, for once correctly played as a sexually aware and even seductive teenager, had a forcefulness and energy that directors usually edit out of the role, and for which Michael Stuhlbarg's Ferdinand, played as a cheerful, preppy naval cadet, served as a perfect foil. The sexual dynamics, in fact, were interestingly subversive: Stuhlbarg is a nice-looking actor (he was Demetrius in Scheie's *Midsummer Night's Dream*), but his Ferdinand was distinctly less attractive than either Ariel or Caliban. Schulman's Miranda remained sexually in control.

Scheie has always been fascinated by the possibilities offered by both doubling and gender crossing in Shakespearean theater. In his *Comedy of Errors*, not only the twins were doubled, but the duke reappeared (in yellow lounging pajamas) as the courtesan. In *A Midsummer Night's Dream*, Theseus and Hippolyta doubled chiastically with Oberon and Titania—Hippolyta made a stylish Oberon, Garbo in drag, while Theseus, a powerful figure with a military bearing, was preposterously funny as Titania in a white tutu and blonde curls. In Scheie's *Merchant of Venice*, Bassanio was played by a woman, who doubled, moreover, as Morocco and Aragon (so that Portia kept getting the same man, who wasn't even a man), and the gender-bending had a particular force: both Jessica's and Antonio's escapes from Shylock, after all, depend on the ability of women to perform as men. The fluidity of gender in Scheie's productions unquestionably has its shock value, but it also helps to remind us that Shakespeare's theater is one in which both women and men are gendered entirely through performance. Young men become women if they are dressed as women, and nobody ever sees through Rosalind's, Portia's,

Viola's, or Imogen's male disguises. In Scheie's *Tempest*, the genders themselves remained for the most part undisturbed, though Ariel camped up his female roles amusingly (Newton was a glamorous and remarkably convincing Olivia in Scheie's all-male *Twelfth Night*). But the polymorphous quality of the play's sexuality was always in evidence: Prospero's and Ariel's feeling for each other was unmistakable, and Zerbe's Caliban, even at his most farcical moments, had a powerful homoerotic charge.

The decision to double the crucial family members—Prospero with Antonio, Alonso with Ferdinand—creates obvious problems in Act 5, when everyone is on stage together. But the idea turned out to have its points: Irwin Appel without the fright wig made Antonio a figure of malevolent formality in a black business suit; the zany energy was, in this incarnation, still there, but scarily under control. Michael Stuhlbarg's Ferdinand doubling as his father Alonso was a grown-up preppy, like Clive Brook in *Shanghai Express.* Instead of using stand-ins at the play's conclusion, Scheie employed dummies. This worked better in the case of Antonio, a huge rag doll whom Prospero finally simply tossed offstage in disgust at his refusal to repent—the wicked brother's unregeneracy is perfectly unambiguous in the text, but most directors prefer to fudge it. Alonso's ventriloquized dialogue with Ferdinand as a department store dummy was harder to bring off, but the articulate and vibrant Miranda concluding the play betrothed to a wooden doll is not entirely untrue to the text.

Scheie's handling of the masque was strikingly successful. Directors generally consider this scene an embarrassment and either radically trim it or cut it entirely. Here it was what it is in Shakespeare, the centerpiece of the play, the most palpable example we are shown of Prospero's art. This Prospero presented a divine beauty pageant, with the three goddesses in sequined ball gowns vying for first place, and the nymphs clowning up the poetry by producing props that realize the imagery—Quaker Oats, Wonder Bread, a bottle of rye, etc. The sight gags were corny, but the result was genuinely funny; and for once Miranda and Ferdinand were seen to be enjoying themselves at their betrothal masque. But the most remarkable thing in the production was its ability to produce moments of seriousness: Appel's "Ye elves of hills" speech was beautifully pronounced, a moment of genuine magic in the lunacy of the comedy; Ariel, persuading his master to renounce his vengeance, descended from his trapeze, touchingly, into Prospero's arms; Caliban, vowing to seek for grace hereafter, was reconciled with Prospero in a sudden, startling, utterly convincing embrace. At these moments the zany farce became genuinely moving—Scheie's *Tempest* was a comedy of wonder and delight.

In 2000 Scheie returned to Santa Cruz to do a fascinating and brilliant *Cymbeline*. Modern audiences and critics obviously have less invested in the seriousness of *Cymbeline* than in that of *The Tempest*, and the comic turns and running gags that filled this production were largely responsible for its success. That this involved some artistic license goes without saying: the play on the page is not notably comic—indeed, in the folio, it appears as a tragedy. Doubtless this primarily reflects the difficulty the folio's editors were having in categorizing it, since the only available options were comedy, history, and tragedy, and the play more or less fits all three, but comfortably fits none. If the folio had included a section of tragicomedies, *Cymbeline* would surely have gone there. So, however, would the comedies *Measure for Measure, All's Well That Ends Well, The Winter's Tale*, and perhaps even *Much Ado About Nothing* and *The Merchant of Venice*—Shakespeare's notions of comedy and tragedy are anything but pure. Still, one would have thought that all those averted disasters, repentances, concluding reconciliations, the recovery of the lost sons, the fact that nobody dies except the villains, and the ultimate reunions not only of Imogen and Posthumus but even of England and Rome in the time of universal peace would have qualified it as a comedy. The trouble is that unlike *The Winter's Tale*, which is the Shakespeare play it most resembles, there really is not much in *Cymbeline* to laugh at. The ending is upbeat, certainly, but if there are to be laughs, they must be imported—there isn't even a clown in it.

So to begin with, Scheie's *Cymbeline* was unlike Shakespeare's in that it was very funny. The setting, a simple architectural façade, was surmounted by a bank of video monitors that played a running visual commentary, for the most part parodic and subversive. Costumes were largely modern, though modernity here ranged from the thirties to the seventies, and consistency was never an issue: there were pure fairy-tale outfits for the king and queen, and when Posthumus and his Italian friends became an invading Roman army, they were dressed like Julie Taymor's soldiers in *Titus*. In one sense the production was a send-up of the play, but in another sense, it really was taking the play on its own terms: tragedy or not, *Cymbeline* is very difficult to take seriously. If it isn't funny, much of it is loony, or idiotic, or baffling; and in that case—for a modern theater, at least—it had better be funny. Play Shylock straight, and *The Merchant of Venice* approaches tragedy; but play the Queen and Cloten straight, and *Cymbeline* is simply preposterously melodramatic. Imogen's trials and transformations and multiple fake deaths, moreover, are the stuff of fairy tales, not tragedy. Scheie's comedy was in fact very revealing about the dynamics of the play—about what *can* be taken seriously in it. The theatrical strategies of the production were characteristically startling, often disconcerting, sometimes frankly outrageous; but they seemed to me more often right than wrong, and indeed, sometimes produced genuine revelations.

For example, Cloten's deep, pervasive, continuous indignation after Imogen invidiously compares him with Posthumus's "meanest garment" (II.3.133) was played as a running gag, but it also became a touchstone, a potent index to the character. In this production, it was Cloten who could not let go of the gag, not the play. Cloten is usually played as utterly repulsive, physically gross as well as morally repellent; this is what Imogen's reaction to him seems to require. Scheie made him instead petulant and silly, but not at all unattractive; and this seemed to me true to the play—in fact, I would have made him more attractive still. Imogen, after all, has to mistake him physically for Posthumus, and when she wakes and finds him and describes his headless body, it seems to her positively godlike—"his foot Mercurial, his Martial thigh,/The brawns of Hercules" (IV.2.310–311): he is perfectly gorgeous.

Liam Vincent is a very good comedian, but his way of playing Cloten did systematically disarm his villainy—for all the threats and invective, he was clearly not at all dangerous, and in his one physical encounter, with Guiderius, he was played here as a hopeless coward. This certainly worked theatrically, but it also simplified the play, and there was a way in which it was a missed opportunity. Scheie conceived his Iachimo as a tough, smolderingly sexy thug, beautifully played by Andy Murray. Suppose Cloten had been conceived that way, to make clear just how dangerously attractive sex is in the play? In Scheie's *Tempest*, the wonderfully magnetic and charismatic Jack Zerbe was a complex, erotic, and moving Caliban. I would have welcomed some of that complexity in Cloten. The headless-corpse scene is an astonishing moment, not least because it requires us to reconsider just how different the loathsome, murderous rapist really is from the adored, idealized husband: they turn out, at this moment, to be all but identical, so similar that Imogen cannot tell them apart. The production had a kind of manic energy, much of which was frankly sexual, and the confusion of Cloten and Posthumus really needed to be at the center of the play.

Susannah Schulman's Imogen was vivacious, glamorous, and enthusiastic, all clinging dresses and long hair. Hans Altwies's Posthumus was classically handsome, clean-cut, and impeccably turned out in crisp seersucker. Initially they might have been a couple out of a Noel Coward comedy. And the rival suitor Cloten seemed everything Posthumus was not: not only boastful, coarse, foolish, insensitive, and arrogant but also hilariously badly dressed in khaki shorts and a Union Jack shirt; most to the point, he was lecherous and very persistent. Posthumus, banished to Rome, however, moved not merely from England to Italy but from 1930s romantic comedy to *Goodfellas* or *The Sopranos*, and here the antithesis between the suitors quickly started to blur. The meeting with Philario and Iachimo took place in a pool hall. Iachimo, in black leather, bare-armed and tattooed, effortlessly taunted Posthumus into gambling with Imogen's chastity, effortlessly elicited his permission to try to seduce her. Posthumus's compliance, too easily obtained, is obviously far more dangerous and destructive than Cloten's clumsy attempts at wooing; but though Imogen subsequently sees through Iachimo's strategy almost at once, she also, surprisingly, forgives him almost at once. Her graciousness in Scheie's production seemed, if anything, rather overdone—she has passed the test, but she also hasn't been entirely displeased by this attempt on her virtue. And Andy Murray then played the midnight-bedroom scene with a clear sense that he has already won. For all his evident lechery, his real satisfaction consisted in the collection of evidence and the prospect of facing Posthumus down; in pocketing the bracelet, the ring, the money. This is, of course, just how Posthumus has set things up, in making the bracelet and the ring stand for Imogen's chastity. In fact, as it turns out, Iachimo hardly needs the evidence: back in Rome, Posthumus is all too ready to believe him.

In the mafioso world of Scheie's Rome, the transition from adoring husband to murderous dupe was strikingly logical, and Altwies's furious revelation

of how far from ideal the marriage with Imogen actually was—"Me of my law-
ful pleasure she oft restrained/And bade me oft forbearance" (II.5.9–10)—came
as a sufficient explanation for both his compliance in the wager and his rage
at its outcome. These difficult scenes were beautifully realized, and they maintained their seriousness within the predominantly comic and satiric context.
The denial of sexuality also explained, if more conventionally, the translation
of Imogen into Fidele: in standard Renaissance plots, women dress as youths to
avoid unwanted sexual encounters—though the play immediately renders the
strategy problematic when Guiderius and Arviragus declare their homoerotic
passion for the newly created Fidele, a plot twist that is short-circuited only by
the presumed death of the beloved young man.

Scheie's most startling directorial decision was to signal Posthumus's
emergence as the British hero by sending him into battle totally naked. This
was designed to be outrageous, which it certainly was: Posthumus did not
merely flash us; he was naked for a good ten minutes. It was also hilarious, and
exciting, and in its way entirely apt: it made the idealization of Posthumus not
only blatant, but blatantly sexual—Altwies looked great without his clothes.
If the play is going to end in reconciliation, this is the Posthumus Imogen has
to accept; this is what Imogen has to accept about Posthumus. And though
this bit of sensational theatrics was all Scheie's, the play does toy with just this
kind of revelation. When the Imogen of Shakespeare's stage in 1609 started
to undress and said "I . . . am almost/A man already" (III.4.167–168), how
far did she go— how far was almost? There is a similar moment in *Othello*,
when Desdemona undresses for bed: how far did Shakespeare's Desdemona
go? Neither could have gone as far as Susannah Schulman's Imogen, who went
down to bra and panties, quite far enough to demonstrate that she was in
fact a woman, because for Shakespeare's Imogen or Desdemona to have gone
that far would have revealed just the opposite, the man beneath the dress—to
undress, in this theater, was to prove you were male.

Gender, like office and class in Shakespeare's theater, is a function of costume: a woman is anyone who wears a dress, a man anyone who wears trousers, a soldier a man in armor, a king a man with a crown—and Posthumus
is a dead body in Posthumus's clothes; nobody ever sees through a disguise
in Shakespeare.[2] So the proof that Iachimo has really been with Imogen has

to be a bodily proof, the mole on her breast; and the proof that Polydore is really Guiderius is a birthmark, the evidence of his body. Stripping Posthumus naked was not simply a piece of gratuitous porn (though it certainly was that); for once, finally, somebody in this play really was what he seemed. He was not only that, of course; even the naked Posthumus had his patriotic signifier, a Union Jack in grease paint adorning his chest, all too clearly recalling Cloten's Union Jack shirt. But the rest of his signifiers were unabashedly anatomical; clothes for once did not make the man.

This was a directorial decision, not at all required by the script; but it was a decision that has become almost a cliché of recent theater, and often with much less point. In 1995, on Broadway, Jude Law took a very leisurely onstage bath, frequently standing up, for much of Act 2 of Cocteau's *Les Parents Terribles* (absurdly retitled *Indiscretions*, apparently in deference to the supposed linguistic incompetence of New Yorkers). The script calls only for the actor to enter from the bathroom in bare feet, but the play was running in competition with Terence McNally's *Love! Valor! Compassion!* (of which Vincent Canby, reviewing the play in the *New York Times*, said "it offers more male nudity than has probably ever been seen in a legitimate Broadway theater"[3]), and Jude Law's talents were obviously too good to waste on mere acting—Law had also been nude in the London production, where there was no anatomical competition. San Francisco was only a step behind: the next season, in the American Conservatory Theater's *Othello*, a dignified but distinctly dumpy Othello undressed and took an extended bath in the middle of an early conversation with Iago; and a year later the ACT's *Duchess of Malfi* stripped the duchess naked for her death scene and left her lying on a gurney for most of the last act, while her brother Ferdinand performed his lycanthropic scene also naked. All these roles were performed by actors who, not to put too fine a point on it, looked a great deal better in their costumes than out of them. In 2000 ACT finally got its anatomical act together with Mark Lamos's production of *Edward II*, in which practically everybody was nude for long periods (sex does, after all, figure significantly in the play). The casting must have been done in a gym: all the actors were stunning. I was surprised that they could actually read lines too.

The naked hero made a real conceptual sense in Scheie's *Cymbeline*. One of the great pleasures in all Scheie's productions is everything beside the

acting—what one might call the undertones: the allusive decor, the implied subtext, the ironic background. Sight gags, sound gags, technological gimmicks,
puppets, animations, and anachronisms provide a running commentary that
drives people for whom Shakespeare is The Canon crazy, and drives people for
whom Shakespeare is the essence of theater crazy with joy. When the queen's
death was announced, the opening bars of "Ding, dong, the witch is dead"
were heard. The Jupiter section of Holst's *The Planets* was ubiquitous throughout the latter half of the play; indeed, the finale, the treacly patriotic hymn
"I Vow to Thee My Country" is set to the Jupiter theme and had every expa-
triate Briton in the audience—a large group in Santa Cruz—singing along
(it was Princess Diana's favorite hymn and was sung at both her wedding
and her funeral). Beethoven's Pastoral Symphony signaled Imogen's arrival in
Wales, where Belarius and the princes were a minuscule boy scout troop and
the cave was their pup tent. The opening notes of Beethoven's overture to
Fidelio were heard whenever Imogen declared that her name was Fidele (this
only happens three times, but that was once too many). The aria "Casta diva"
("Chaste goddess") from Bellini's opera *Norma* was the background music for
Imogen going to bed—*Norma*, like *Cymbeline*, is set in ancient Britain—and
there were, during the Roman invasion, appropriate bits from Handel's *Julius
Caesar*, and, as the plot works itself out, Beethoven's variations on *God Save the
King*. I got this far myself; a companion who is not generationally challenged
as I am pointed out the Sex Pistols singing their version of *God Save the Queen*,
Annette Funicello on how much she likes Italians when Posthumus first got
to Rome, and a little bell with its accompanying freeze-frame action from the
television series *Bewitched*, which served as a running gag throughout. During
the Italian scenes the video monitors played RAI news in Italian, and, during
the Roman invasion, in Latin—a neat way of registering how the play switches
back and forth between modern Italy and ancient Rome.

As for the visual gags, Imogen, when she goes to bed, is reading Ovid: the
book here was the Riverside Shakespeare, with the name Ovid pasted across it.
The tablet that Posthumus awoke to find after his dream, and from which he
and Stephen Grenley's marvelously campy soothsayer read Jove's prophecy, was
a copy of the Arden edition of *Cymbeline*. The television monitors offered, as
a running commentary, clips of Edward VIII and Mrs. Simpson, scenes from

Mrs. Thatcher's Britain, odd bits of the Beatles, Elizabeth Taylor as Cleopatra, *Upstairs Downstairs* upside down. Imogen heading off to Wales was glossed on the tiny screens by Julie Andrews in *The Sound of Music* and Samantha Eggar in *Dr. Doolittle* making their breaks for freedom. Allusively, the production was distinctly nostalgic (who even remembers Samantha Eggar?); but the nostalgia was all over the place: the 30s, the 50s, the 70s: there was something corny for everyone—at least, for everyone over forty. There were sight gags on stage too: Andy Murray's Iachimo, the mafioso thug, kept his fingers crossed when apologizing to Imogen; Tommy Gomez's scoutmaster Belarius gave a visible sigh of relief when he realized he did not have two gay scouts in his troop after all; the beefeater jailer guarding Posthumus was drinking Beefeater gin. Amy Thone's marvelous, unflappable wicked queen was a running visual gag: the primary butt was Mrs. Thatcher wielding a gold purse, but a dress with a huge angel-wing collar recalled Elizabeth I's Rainbow Portrait, and there were moments of Elizabeth II as well. The video screens glossed her poisoning attempts with Beatrice Lillie in *Thoroughly Modern Millie*. The production had both total recall and a very subversive sense of relevance.

The problem with taking the comedy of tragicomedy seriously is that it makes it so difficult to keep the tragic element in view, and that remained a problem here. One could argue that the problem is built into the form: the point about tragicomedy is not that it is both tragic and comic, but that it is really neither; the comedy undercuts the tragedy, the tragedy subverts the restorations and reconciliations. Scheie's *Cymbeline* did have its transcendent moments; but I wanted a few more. The most serious loss for me was in the way Cymbeline's response to the revelation of the queen's villainy was handled in the last act. Cymbeline says,

>   Mine eyes
> Were not in fault, for she was beautiful,
> Mine ears that heard her flattery, nor my heart
> That thought her like her seeming. It had been vicious
> To have mistrusted her; yet, O my daughter,
> That it was folly in me thou mayst say,
> And prove it in thy feeling. Heaven mend all! (V.5.63–69)

Gary Armagnac pretty much threw this away, but it seems to me a really crucial moment in the play. These lines say that untrustworthy as appearances are, they are all we have to base our trust on. This is a comment on the whole nature of perception in the play—Imogen says, "Our very eyes/Are sometimes, like our judgments, blind" (IV.2.301–302), and it is impossible to know whether she means that our judgments are sometimes blind or always blind; but in any case the benchmark for blindness is judgment, not eyesight. How do you ever know what is true? In fact, the play makes very little distinction between lies and truth. When Pisanio is questioned about the disappearance of Imogen, he is exculpated by one of Shakespeare's omniscient Gentlemen, who testifies that Pisanio was at court on the day Imogen was missing, and therefore cannot be implicated in her disappearance. This is a flat lie, and it comes from the same Gentleman who reports the Roman invasion: he is there to do nothing but give information. (Scheie rationalized this moment by giving the lie instead to Imogen's maid, who would have a reason for covering for Pisanio.)

Cymbeline is certainly as bad a king as we find in Shakespeare—as bad as Lear or Leontes, irascible, gullible, vain, arbitrary, unjust—but he is, like Lear and Leontes, nevertheless the king, and he is at the center of this society. When Posthumus is in prison, he has a vision of his dead family, who, in a resumé of the action, question the possibility of justice in a world such as the play presents. In reply, Jove descends and offers a version of divine justice that is simply Cymbeline's justice writ large: "Whom best I love, I cross" (V.4.101). There *is* a divine order, but it is much larger and more impersonal than anything we can comprehend, and it does not take human suffering into account—Jove's love produces only pain; God's love leads to the cross. This may be a basis for reconciliation (it is, after all, God's love), but it is not a recipe for a happy ending; and the folio editors considered the play a tragedy. Posthumus's dream appeared here on the video screens, with Hans Altwies playing all his relatives, including, in drag, his mother, and with a crazily animated Jupiter and eagle descending—to the theme, naturally, from Mozart's Jupiter Symphony. This had a Monty Pythonish energy and wit, but the larger point pretty much got lost.

One of the great pleasures of watching Scheie's productions over the years is seeing how he manages to transform a group of actors with quite individual acting styles into a unified troupe. Part of what makes this possible is that his conception of theater is so frankly anarchic, and disparity is part of the mix. But part of it is really the other side of this anarchy: Shakespearean drama has far more energy than any single reading, any one interpretation, can accommodate, and there are very few directors who are willing to let that energy play out in the theater. Nobody has ever made *Cymbeline* funny in this way; but also nobody else has been willing to acknowledge the genuine craziness of Shakespeare's conception, to do the play and remain true to its manic energy.

—(1995/2000)

Shakespeare all'italiana

In early July 2005, when I was in Rome with the Italian Renaissance scholar Michael Wyatt, *La Reppublica* reported on a fashion show. Such a news item would not ordinarily have attracted our attention, but the show was being held in the Globe Theater in the gardens of the Villa Borghese. A Roman Globe was unknown to us—its full name is the Silvano Toti Globe Theater, and it opened in 2003. A production of *Romeo e Giulietta* was scheduled for a few days later, and we put together a theater party of six, including three Italian friends.

The theater is located in what is otherwise a poet's corner for foreign writers—one walks to Shakespeare past life-sized statues of Pushkin, Gogol, the Persian poet Nizami, the Inca Garcilaso de la Vega. The theater itself is in a little grove, scarcely visible from the path; its unpretentiousness and lack of publicity, for someone who has recently been in London—where one is deluged with enticements to what is preposterously called "Shakespeare's Globe"—are very striking. The Roman theater is indeed modeled on the original Globe, an octagonal timbered building of stucco and wood, and it was built as part of the centenary celebrations of the Villa Borghese. Silvano Toti was a construction magnate with an interest in the arts; he died in 1989, leaving money for a cultural foundation, and it was this that funded the project. The construction of the theater took three months—*three months*. This is about the time it took to build the original Globe. In contrast, the construction of London's new theater consumed years, and many millions. The Roman Globe explicitly disclaims any attempt at authenticity; its publicity brochure observes, disarmingly and accurately, that the theater "must not be considered an imitation of [the 1599 Globe], for which indeed, there is no extant copy of the original plan." It also observes that "the theater, which reproduces the characteristic great wooden O of the original, aims at being a space for both the creativity and fantasy of Italian and foreign artists within a multidisciplinary perspective," and concludes, unidiomatically but charmingly, that this Globe is "also a stage suited for Elizabethan stagings which take advantage of the happy essence of the architectural plan."

The interior dimensions of the theater are about the same as those of London's Globe, though it holds far fewer people, with a capacity of only 1,250 (as opposed to London's 3,000); 420 of these are groundlings. It has a simple, unadorned thrust stage with a curtained discovery space and a large gallery above. The seating is on three levels and is even more uncomfortable than it is in London, on wooden benches without backs; but the sight lines are far better in Rome: the massive columns supporting the roof in London, which obstruct the view from most of the side seats (and derive not from any evidence about the Globe but from the surviving drawing of the Swan theater), in Rome are unobtrusive timber supports, which serve on occasion as trees or other scenic elements. In Silvano Toti's Globe, there is no reason to insist on a center seat; the stage is genuinely open, and one sees well from everywhere.

The Roman theater is better for groundlings, too. In London, because of the fire laws, standees in the pit are forbidden to sit on the ground—on a hot day (or during a boring production) the discomfort is palpable, and performances are preceded by both warnings and apologies. Rome has fire laws too, but the groundlings are welcome to make themselves comfortable by crouching or sitting: safety is assured by the presence of a good-natured group of burly firemen in full gear, who lounge about visibly at the sides of the auditorium and stroll through the pit during intermissions. The general effect is of an incipient bit of *Much Ado About Nothing* hovering constantly in the wings.

As for the quality of the acoustics, it was difficult to tell, because, unlike the practice of the London Globe, everything is miked. This is probably not entirely necessary: for about ten minutes during *Romeo e Giulietta* Romeo's microphone stopped working, and he was perfectly audible, even when he was facing away from us—this is not the case in London's Globe. The major disadvantage of the amplification is that it is too uniform, and subtleties of tone disappear; but weighing this against the amount of lost dialogue on London's Bankside, one often felt grateful for the microphones. Doubtless a more sophisticated amplification system could be installed; but one of the charms of the Roman Globe is precisely its unpretentiousness.

Romeo e Giulietta was performed without sets and with very few props, the principal one being a large trunk, which for the wedding night scene served as Juliet's bed, and was then her dowry chest, her bier, and finally her tomb. The cast was young and energetic, and played beautifully as an ensemble. Costumes were simple: black tights for most of the men, more elaborate dresses, mainly black, for the women. There were a few spots of color—red for the prince, white for the lovers in the wedding scene—but the production remained visually very simple. The performance, however, was complex and exciting, with very fast pacing; the performing time was just two and a half hours, using a text with no major cuts. Romeo (the only member of the cast with movie-star good looks) was a gymnast, running, leaping, climbing up the balcony, nearly always in motion. Giulietta, in a strikingly original performance, looked and acted thirteen. The role, played in this way, made superb sense, and passages that in anglophone productions are commonly cut or truncated, such as Juliet's potion speech, worked beautifully here: the hyperbolic fears were the imagination of innocence and inexperience, and the melodramatic rhetoric came naturally from a thirteen-year-old—for once in this scene, nobody laughed. Mercutio was superb. The Queen Mab speech, beautifully recited, was played very physically and at a high-pitched psychological level; his companions seemed completely mesmerized by the performance, so that Romeo's interruption gave the sense of a spell being broken. The Nurse, who was not elderly, but looked to be in her thirties (in the text, she need be no more than twenty-eight: she had a daughter the same age as Juliet, who was born when Lady Capulet was fourteen), played the role throughout in a tightly wound emotional state, almost as a hysteric, so that the instant reversal, her abandonment of Juliet ("Marry Paris; Romeo's a dishclout to him") made perfect sense—she was always very close to being out of control, and the performance gave an unusual sense of how dangerous she is in the play, how dependent Juliet is on her, and how ultimately unreliable she is. Juliet's father, in contrast, was very reasonable, not only when the subject of Juliet's marriage to Paris was first proposed, but in relation to the family feud generally; and when he went out of control after Tybalt's death the transformation was all the more powerful.

These actors were not in awe of the text and made theatrical capital out of things that English productions are typically embarrassed by and cut—Juliet's potion speech was the most striking example, but almost as surprising was Friar Laurence's first scene, invariably a bore on the anglophone stage, which was here performed uncut, and at the conclusion received enthusiastic applause. The translation seemed to stay close to the English, and the sonnets remained sonnets, though the Italian speakers among us also noted a certain amount of current slang. The music, oddly, was Elgar.

The director of this thrilling production was the brilliant and prolific Gigi Proietti, who had been active in the Italian theater for more than forty years (he died in 2020), and here deliberately assembled a young and largely unknown cast. A search of the internet revealed that by 2005 the glamorous, athletic Romeo, Alessandro Averone, had starred in a short film made in Croatia in 2002 and appeared in a full-length film that won a prize at the Montreal film festival in 2004; in addition, he had a single professional stage credit. The extraordinary Giulietta, Valentina Marziali, had been in an Italian production of *Much Ado*, and in one TV film. On the web the great Mercutio, Alessandro Albertin, had no stage credits at all, and appeared only as the co-author of a play. Nadia Rinaldi, the Nurse, had done a good deal of TV; Friar Laurence, Massimiliano Giovannetti, had made two films. There were star turns in this production, but no stars.[1]

A month later we returned for *La Dodicesima Notte*, *Twelfth Night*, by the same company, but directed by Riccardo Cavallo, and with an entirely different cast, which was again, with one exception, largely unknown. This production was marvelous, even better than *Romeo e Giulietta* because it was more inventive and adventurous (and the budget was clearly somewhat larger).[2] It was also quite freewheeling: to begin with, the company did not understand the title at all. "La dodicesima notte," though it is standard in all Italian translations of the play, is not a possible translation of Twelfth Night. In English, Twelfth Night refers only to the feast of Epiphany, the sixth of January (the twelfth night of the Christmas season)—the relevance of the title to the play has been much debated, but its invocation of both the season of feasting and revelry and the concept of revelation, epiphany, is clearly appropriate. "La dodicesima notte" translates into English as *the* twelfth night, with a definite article, and simply means the twelfth in any sequence of nights—nothing to do with Epiphany at all. A correct Italian version of the title would be *L'Epifanìa*, just as, in French, the play is called *La Nuit des Rois*. Cavallo and his actors missed the reference, took the title in its numerical sense, and interpreted the story as an Arabian Nights tale, making this the twelfth of the 1,001 nights. So it was presented in a kind of fairy tale oriental dress, understated but quite beautiful. Sir Andrew was the one exception, in a turquoise variety of Scots tartan, including kilt and beret. Presumably this was an allusion to St. Andrew, the patron saint of Scotland, though his name in the production was Sir Andrea. The presence of a Scot in Illyria, especially a turquoise one, made little sense, but it added to the air of exoticism.

The décor was vaguely Moorish. There were two small reflecting pools with fountains and two minimalist screens, which remained onstage and were used variously throughout. In this languidly sensuous setting, the sexual innuendo of the play became overt. For the opening scene, Orsino recited "If music be the food of love" while lying on the floor with his servant Valentine, who became Valentina in this production; they were making love. She was bare-breasted, and though he kept his trousers on, it was clear that sex was in progress. So all the praise of Olivia served as a way of getting themselves excited—Valentina enjoys being the go-between; and whenever she returns from her invariably fruitless errands, they make fun of Olivia. They clearly both get a charge out of this. Similarly, later, in Cesario's first scene in Orsino's court, Valentina has her speech about how quickly he has become the new favorite, but in this production she felt him up while reciting it and tried to kiss him. This in fact addresses a problem in the play, about why Cesario's sudden preferment in the household evokes no jealousy. Valentina's attempt to co-opt the new favorite by making a lover out of him made emotional sense, and dramatically worked very well. More was made of the difficulty of maintaining the cross-dressing than is usual in anglophone productions—in the lead-up to "She never told her love," Orsino walked in on Cesario bathing in one of the pools, though he was so self-involved that he didn't take a close enough look to catch the reason for his servant's embarrassment as Cesario grabbed for a robe and, quite naked to the audience, ran across the stage and dressed behind one of the tiny pillars (which of course did not conceal her at all).

As for Olivia, she was played as a kind of society dumbbell, whose love for Cesario comes out of nowhere and about whom everything is exaggeratedly emotional—a figure who would not be out of place in *Dallas* or *Dynasty* (or the Italian soap opera *Un Posto al Sole*). She falls for Cesario because she falls for everyone, except, perversely, the one person who wants her—or says he does— Orsino. Orsino was played as very energetic and forceful, but about nothing, completely unfocused—the continuing love affair with Valentina had much more sense of direction than the supposed love for Olivia, or, in the end, than what he professed for Viola: he was Mr. Big from *Sex and the City*, a creature of the moment, indulging whatever passion took his fancy.

The comic characters Sir Toby, Sir Andrew, Maria, and Feste (Fabian was cut) had the air of old-style vaudevillians among a cast of ingenues. Their performances were, on the whole, the strongest and most professional in the production, and the director used them superbly. One had a sense that, among all these aimless aristocrats, here was one group of characters with both a sense of purpose and a sense of style, louche and raucous but consistent, and consistently funny. The drunken revel of the confrontation with Malvolio, the "Cakes and ale" scene, was cut and replaced with a miniature Rossini farce, ten minutes of brilliant, wild invention harnessing the drunken energy to music—the music sounded like real Rossini to me, though apparently it was a pastiche. It was a superb one, totally convincing. Suddenly the play belonged to the clowns—this is what one longs for in the comic scenes, but no anglophone production could get away with this sort of really daring substitution: English performers and audiences are simply too much in awe of the Shakespeare text. These comedians played together beautifully and often were clearly driving the show; much of the energy of the performance came from them. Sir Toby carried a wine bottle throughout as an attribute. When the twins finally appeared together, he decided he was seeing double, and stumbled across the stage to stow the bottle in one of the pools. A few minutes later, when the doubling was explained, he retrieved the bottle—a nice gag, but also an emblem of how flimsy conversions are in the play.

The pompous and self-conscious Malvolio was one of the best I have ever seen, again brilliantly directed. In the letter scene, to begin with, he had a lot of trouble retrieving the letter—it was stuck to his shoe because of the wax seal. Reading it, he began with a word of gibberish, repeated several times; then, with a sudden recognition, he turned the letter upside down, and the word came out right. (When Olivia was given the letter in the final scene, the joke was repeated.) As Malvolio read the letter, Sir Toby and the conspirators hid behind one of the pool screens, gesticulating, and staying out of sight with difficulty—when Malvolio stumbled over the meaning of MOAI, Sir Andrew ran out to explain it to him and had to be dragged back by Maria. Wearing a capacious caftan and a turban, grand-vizier style, this Malvolio was certainly not what Maria calls him, a kind of puritan, but he was a quintessential bureau-crat, parading his authority but revealing nothing except his ambition. The yellow cross-gartered stockings were a surprise, quite invisible until he pulled up his gown to reveal them (so that being required to wear them was singularly pointless). The smiling that accompanied the garters was more than a smile, a compulsive "ho ho ho," very disconcerting to the dizzy Olivia, constituting yet another event in the play that seemed beyond her control or understanding. In the prison scene, Malvolio was placed under an open trapdoor, perfectly visible and not in darkness. Feste, however, in a kind of domino, was unrecognizable, miming a deep, oracular voice, disturbing and not at all comic. That scene seemed to come out of nowhere—the introductory dialogue with Sir Toby explaining its point was cut—so that it really only served to justify Malvolio's vengefulness at the end. And the vengefulness in this production was uncom-promising: when Malvolio stalked out, he did not just stalk offstage, he walked through the audience and clear out of the theater, so there could be no question of pursuing him and making peace. He was gone.

Antonio and Sebastian, the latter young and very attractive, the former middle-aged, were played as overtly gay, but Sebastian seemed to want to move on, nervous about it. Nevertheless, in the recognition scene, when you thought he was going to run to embrace his sister Viola, now unmasked, he instead rushed past her and into Antonio's arms—this is in the text: Sebastian, catching sight of his friend in the last scene, cries "Antonio, O my dear Antonio,/How have the hours racked and tortured me/Since I have lost thee!" (5.1.213–215), a declaration of continuing love that few anglophone directors can handle. For the finale, when Olivia and Orsino decide they will be as brother and sister, Orsino kissed both Olivia's hands, and then, very slowly, with Sebastian and Viola looking on dumbfounded, they went into a deep kiss, which they held throughout Feste's final song. That long kiss was how the play ended.

In this cast, only Sir Toby, Roberto Della Casa, had a substantial number of acting credits, all, to judge from the internet, in film and television. The brilliant Malvolio, Nicola d'Eramo, had appeared in only three films, including a small part in the original *La Cage aux Folles*. Claudia Balboni, the wonderful Olivia, had been in five stage productions, and is also a director and costumer. The rest of the impeccably professional cast proved to be similarly elusive. Once again, this was a company, not a star turn. It was certainly the most interesting *Twelfth Night* I have ever seen, and one reason it was so strikingly successful was that it took seriously the play's hesitations, surprises, and reversals—Orsino instantly proposing marriage to Viola rather than to Olivia; Olivia effortlessly transferring her affections from Cesario to Sebastian; Sebastian transferring his from Antonio to Olivia, and seemingly, at the last moment, back again. In *Hamlet*, written in the same year as *Twelfth Night*, the notion that brothers might be erotically interchangeable is the precipitating subject of the tragedy: the chronicle of Olivia's effortless change of heart is the real play within the play in *Hamlet*. Nor does *Twelfth Night* conclude with what it seems to promise, a group of happy marriages, that defining staple of comedy: the plot, in fact, does not conclude at all, but opens out in its final moments onto a world of new confusions. No anglophone production can ever deal with the ending Shakespeare gives us, which makes the return and reconciliation of Malvolio a prerequisite to the marriage of Orsino and Viola—Shakespeare's script, in an entirely unanticipated plot twist, aborts the traditional comic conclusion. This is a bit of plotting that materializes in the last two minutes of the action, and it needs to be insisted upon because not only performances, but critical accounts of the play, normally ignore it.

Riccardo Cavallo, in contrast, made dramatic capital out of it, so that the finale was one of the most original and compelling moments in the performance.

The concluding moments of the play are concerned as much with the plot against Malvolio as with the sorting out of the marriages. Here is what happens in Shakespeare: Orsino declares that he will marry Viola when he sees her in her "woman's weeds"— this means not simply women's clothing, but her own garments, the costume in which we first saw her after the shipwreck, at the beginning of the play. That costume is Viola; nobody suggests that Viola borrow a dress from Olivia, or buy a new one to get married in. But Viola cannot produce her woman's weeds:

> The captain that did bring me first on shore
> Hath my maid's garments. He upon some action
> Is now in durance, at Malvolio's suit. (5.1.269–271)

The captain is in jail, charged by Malvolio with some nameless offense. It is so that Malvolio can be persuaded to withdraw his action against the captain, so that the captain can then return Viola's clothes, that Olivia orders Malvolio to be brought in—this plot twist seems entirely arbitrary, even pointless, but it is all Shakespeare. Malvolio enters, demanding justice for Olivia's supposed letter and his imprisonment, but Feste, unrepentant, only turns the screw, and the business of the sea captain is not mentioned. Olivia takes Malvolio's side, agreeing that "he hath been most notoriously abused"; but Malvolio, quite understandably, storms off, vowing revenge. It is as much Feste's intransigeance as Malvolio's indignation that has undone the happy ending, and it is to the point that Feste concludes this sunny comedy with his song about the wind and the rain, about how much comic endings leave unsaid. What happens next is *Hamlet*, and the next time Feste's song appears in Shakespeare, the Fool is singing it in the middle of the storm scene in *King Lear.* The end of comedy, Riccardo Cavallo's wonderful production acknowledged, is tragedy.

—(2011)

Notes

INTRODUCTION

1. For an excellent account of the development of Shakespeare's canonicity, see Gary Taylor, *Reinventing Shakespeare* (New York: Weidenfeld and Nicolson, 1989), especially 1–94.

I. THE INVENTION OF SHAKESPEARE

1. *Comedies and Tragedies Written by Francis Beaumont and John Fletcher* (London, 1647), "The Stationer to the Readers," sig. *A4*ʳ.

2. The earliest biography, however, is in John Aubrey's *Brief Lives* (discussed below), compiled 1660–1680, which includes an entry for Shakespeare. Aubrey's manuscript remained unpublished until 1813.

3. Line number references are to the New Pelican edition (New York, Penguin, 2000), edited by Stephen Orgel.

4. A capital S would not be mistaken for an F, but manuscript practice employed capitals rarely and erratically; it was only with printing that the practice began to be standardized.

5. W. Carew Hazlitt, *Remains of the Early Popular Poetry of England* (London: 1866), 2:22.

6. The Chandos portrait, now in the National Portrait Gallery and, since the eighteenth century, widely accepted as the "standard" portrait of Shakespeare, is clearly somebody else. See my *Imagining Shakespeare* (Houndmills: Palgrave Macmillan, 2003), 65–84.

7. *William Shakespeare* by John Aubrey, from *Brief Lives*, edited by Jack Lynch. http://jacklynch.net/Texts/aubrey-shakespeare.html, accessed 10/10/2020.

8. See page 369.

9. Bernice W. Kliman, "At Sea About Hamlet at Sea: A Detective Story," *Shakespeare Quarterly* 62 (2011): 180–204; and Richmond Barbour and Bernhard Klein, "Drama at Sea: A New Look at Shakespeare on the Dragon, 1607–8," in *Travel and Drama in Early Modern England*, ed. Claire Jowitt and David McInnis (Cambridge: Cambridge University Press, 2018), 150–168.

10. Jerzy Limon, *Gentlemen of a Company: English Players in Central and Eastern Europe, 1590–1660* (Cambridge: Cambridge University Press, 1985); Anston Bosman, "Renaissance Intertheater and the Staging of Nobody," *ELH* 71, no. 3 (Fall 2004): 559–585; "Shakespeare and

Globalization," in *The New Cambridge Companion to Shakespeare*, eds. Margreta de Grazia and Stanley Wells (Cambridge: Cambridge University Press, 2010); "Mobility," in *Early Modern Theatricality*, ed. Henry S. Turner (Oxford: Oxford University Press, 2013), 493–515.

11. Lecture on *Hamlet*, January 12, 1812, in J. P. Collier, ed., Samuel Taylor Coleridge, *Seven Lectures on Shakespeare and Milton* (London: Chapman and Hall, 1856), 141–149.

12. *Henry V*, 2.3.16–17.

13. *King Lear*, 4.6.158–159.

14. The fullest and most thoughtful statement of the case is Margreta de Grazia and Peter Stallybrass, "The Materiality of the Shakespearean Text," *Shakespeare Quarterly* 44, no. 3 (Autumn 1993): 255–283. See also my "What Is a Text?" and "The Authentic Shakespeare," both in Stephen Orgel, *The Authentic Shakespeare* (New York: Routledge, 2002), 1–6, 231–256; and Margreta de Grazia, *Shakespeare Verbatim* (Oxford: Oxford University Press, 1991).

2. THE DESIRE AND PURSUIT OF THE WHOLE

1. These are in Francis Meres's *Palladis Tamia: Wit's Treasury* (1598) and a list of books from August 1603 discovered in 1953 in the binding of a volume of sermons. See H. R. Woudhuysen's discussion in his Arden 3 edition of *Love's Labour's Lost* (Walton-on-Thames: Thomas Nelson and Sons, 1998), 78–81.

2. The Master of the Revels records a payment in July 1613 to Shakespeare's company for performing a play at court called *Cardenio*—Cardenio is a character who figures significantly in *Don Quixote*. Or at least, we think that was what the play was called: the record actually gives the title as "Cardenna" and says nothing about it being by Shakespeare. The connection of this lost play with Shakespeare derives from a record made forty years later: the publisher Humphrey Moseley registered his intention to publish a play called "The History of Cardennio," by "Mr Fletcher, and Shakespeare." Moseley never did publish the play; but it is surely relevant that he registered at the same time *The Merry Devil of Edmonton* by "Shakespeare"—this is a play that had been published anonymously in 1608 and in five editions thereafter, and had never been ascribed to Shakespeare. Moseley also registered two other "Shakespeare" plays, *Henry the First* and *Henry the Second*, said to be collaborations with a minor playwright named Robert Davenport, which he also did not publish, and which have, like *Cardenio*, disappeared—Davenport was writing plays in the 1620s and 1630s, long after Shakespeare's death. In 1660, Moseley registered three more plays by "Shakespeare": *The History of King Stephen, Duke Humphrey, A Tragedy*, and *Iphis and Iantha, or a Marriage Without a Man, a Comedy*. Nothing more is known of them; and as for the ascription of any of these plays to Shakespeare, obviously no reliance can be placed on Moseley. But why have we been looking so assiduously for *Cardenio* and ignoring *Henry the First, King Stephen*, and all those others? The only answer probably is that for several centuries we have wanted there to be a connection between Shakespeare and Cervantes. See Michael Dobson, "Shakespeare and Cervantes: Together at Last," *Cervantes—Shakespeare 1616–2016: Contexto, Influencia, Relación / Context, Influence, Relation*, eds. J. M. Gonzalez, J. M. Ferri, and M. del Carmen Irles (Berlin: Edition Reichenberger, [Teatro del Siglo de Oro. Estudios de Literatura; vol. 129]), 9–14.

3. Steevens's comment appears in *The Advertisement to the Plays of William Shakespeare* (1793). See Colin Burrow, ed., Shakespeare, *The Complete Sonnets and Poems* (Oxford: Oxford University Press, 2002), 138.

4. See my essay "No Sense of an Ending" in this volume.

5. July 4, 1857. See Shakespeare, *The Tempest*, ed. Stephen Orgel (Oxford: Clarendon Press, 1987), 72.

6. *Die tragische Geschichte von Hamlet, Prinzen von Dænemark* (Weimar: Cranach Presse, 1929); the English version is J. Dover Wilson, ed., *The Tragedie of Hamlet, Prince of Denmarke* (Weimar: Cranach Press, 1930).

3. NO SENSE OF AN ENDING

1. Sonnet 11. Sir Thomas Wyatt, *Complete Poems*, ed. Ronald Rebholz (London: Penguin Books, 1978), 77.

2. Edmund Spenser, *Amoretti* 30. *Spenser's Minor Poems*, ed. Ernest de Sélincourt (Oxford: Clarendon Press, 1910), 386.

3. Sir Philip Sidney, *Astrophil and Stella* 71. *The Poems*, ed. William A. Ringler (Oxford: Clarendon Press, 1962), 201. In these citations Ringler's fussy, anachronistic, and misleading punctuation has been removed.

4. *Astrophil and Stella* 1. *Poems*, 166.

5. Ibid., 167.

6. *Pause and Effect* (Berkeley: University of California Press, 1993), 305.

7. The forme is the body of type set up to print whatever number of pages will occupy one side of a whole sheet—in the case of a quarto, four pages.

8. Nevertheless, he did not entirely follow orders. The 1609 edition has four italic parentheses; the compositor of 1709 retained only two and, illogically, printed the other two in roman. In addition, because of the catchword on page 69, the 1709 edition includes three sets of parentheses, not two. In the catchword, both parentheses are in roman.

9. William Shakespeare, *The Complete Sonnets and Poems*, ed. Colin Burrow (Oxford: Oxford University Press, 2002), 632.

10. William Shakespeare, *The Sonnets and A Lover's Complaint*, ed. John Kerrigan (London: Penguin Books, 1986), 350–351.

11. See especially Kerrigan's edition, 59, 389–394.

12. Introduction, *Complete Sonnets and Poems*, 139

13. Brian Vickers, *Shakespeare, A Lover's Complaint, and John Davies of Hereford* (Cambridge: Cambridge University Press, 2007).

4. LASCIVIOUS GRACE

1. In Stephen Orgel, *Spectacular Performances* (Manchester: Manchester University Press, 2011), 83–100.

2. *Players of Shakespeare 2*, ed. Russell Jackson and Robert Smallwood (Cambridge: Cambridge University Press, 1988), 179–199.

3. Samuel Pepys, *The Diary of Samuel Pepys*, ed. Robert Latham and William Matthews, vol. 8 (Berkeley: University of California Press, 1974), 7.

4. Dedication to the Epigrams, Ben Jonson, *Workes* (London, 1616), 767.

5. THE POETICS OF INCOMPREHENSIBILITY

Note to epigraph: "A Second Look at Critical Bibliography and the Acting of Plays," *Shakespeare Quarterly* 41 (1990), 87–96. The passage cited is on page 95.

1. Quotations are given in the form in which they appear in the folio, with the letters u, v, i, j, w, and long s normalized. Act, scene, and line numbers are those of the New Pelican edition, eds. Stephen Orgel and A. R. Braunmuller (New York: Penguin, 2002).

2. Quotations from eighteenth- and nineteenth-century editors can be found collected in the *New Variorum Shakespeare: The Winter's Tale*, ed. H. H. Furness (Philadelphia: J. B. Lippincott, 1898).

3. *The Winter's Tale*, in *The Cambridge New Shakespeare*, eds. Arthur Quiller-Couch and John Dover Wilson (Cambridge: Cambridge University Press, 1931), 153.

4. *The Winter's Tale*, ed. J. H. P. Pafford (Arden 2, London: Methuen, 1963), 60.

5. Ibid., 166.

6. See line 361.

7. See, for example, Spenser's *Letter to Ralegh*, Chapman's preface ("To the Understander") to *Achilles' Shield*, and Jonson's preface to *Hymenaei*.

8. The major exception is in biblical commentary, where the glosses bear heavily on interpretive questions deriving from issues raised by the process of translation; the marginalia to the Geneva Bible are a striking instance. Barbara Bono has suggested to me that these constitute a Protestant strategy to counteract Catholic interpretive modes, which were characteristically symbolic and allegorical. There were also a large number of practical texts—handbooks, guides, and the like—that have elucidative glosses. These would naturally depend on clarity for their usefulness. It is to the point that imaginative works are not glossed in this way.

9. See page 131.

10. See page 6.

11. *Ben Jonson His Part of King James His Royal and Magnificent Entertainment*, lines 211–212, in *The Cambridge Ben Jonson*, ed. David Bevington, Martin Butler and Ian Donaldson, vol. 2 (Cambridge: Cambridge University Press, 2012), 441. Quotations from Jonson's works are from this edition.

12. *Hymenaei*, lines 16–17.

13. *Love's Triumph Through Callipolis*, line 1.

14. "I Costumi Teatrali per gli Intermezzi del 1589," *Atti dell'Accademia del Reale Istituto Musicale di Firenze: Commemorazione della Riforma Melodrammatics* (Florence, 1895), 125–126. For a more recent study of an English text with similar conclusions see A. R. Braunmuller, "'To the Globe I Rowed': John Holles Sees *A Game at Chess*," *English Literary Renaissance* 20 (1990), 340–356.

15. 1.2.35–36.

6. TWO HOUSEHOLD FRIENDS

1. Lukas Erne, ed. *The First Quarto of Romeo and Juliet* (Cambridge: Cambridge University Press, 2007). I am also indebted to Jonathan Goldberg's thrilling demolition of spurious bibliographical arguments in "'What? In a Names That Which We Call a Rose,' The Desired Texts of *Romeo and Juliet*," in *Crisis in Editing: Texts of the English Renaissance*, ed. Randall McLeod (New York: AMS Press, 1994), 173–202.

2. For Werstine, see "A Century of 'Bad' Shakespeare Quartos," *Shakespeare Quarterly*, vol. 50, no. 3 (Autumn 1999): 310–333, esp. 326–327 and 332–333.

3. Erne, *First Quarto*, 24.

4. "Shakespeare's Narcissus, Sonnet's Echo," in *The Forms of Renaissance Thought*, ed. Leonard Barkan, Bradin Cormack, and Sean Keilen (Houndmills: Palgrave Macmillan, 2009), 130.

5. Quotations from the two quartos are transcriptions of the original texts, 1597 and 1599.

6. The fifth quarto (1637) also reads "he."

7. Theobald undertook to explain the problem away: "surely, it were easy to say, that no traveller returns to this world, as to his home, or abiding-place," but ignored the information about the afterlife imparted by the Ghost, which Hamlet says we can never know. Coleridge cited the note with approval, S. T. Coleridge *Literary Remains*, ed. H. N. Coleridge (London: Pickering, 1836), 2:227.

8. Samuel Pepys, *The Diary of Samuel Pepys*, ed. Robert Latham and William Matthews, vol. 3 (Berkeley: University of California Press, 1970), 39.

9. George C. Branam, "The Genesis of David Garrick's Romeo and Juliet," *Shakespeare Quarterly* 35.2 (Summer 1984): 170–179.

10. [David Garrick, ed.,],*Romeo and Juliet. By Shakespear. With alterations, and an Additional Scene: As It Is Performed at the Theatre-Royal in Drury-Lane* (London, 1750), sig. A3ʳ.

7. GETTING THINGS WRONG

1. All are cited in H. H. Furness, ed., *A New Variorum Edition of Shakespeare: The Tempest* (Philadelphia: Lippincott, 1892), 86–87.

2. The full argument is in Wilson's Cambridge edition of the play (Cambridge: Cambridge University Press, 1921), 79–85.

3. Frank Kermode, ed., Shakespeare, *The Tempest* (Arden 2: London, Methuen, 1954), 38.

4. For a number of examples and a larger context, see my "The Comedian as the Character 'C,'" *English Comedy*, ed. Michael Cordner, Peter Holland, and John Kerrigan (Cambridge: Cambridge University Press, 1994), 36–54.

5. *Henry V*, 2.3.16–17. The emendation was first proposed in Lewis Theobald, *Shakespeare Restored* (London, 1726), 138, and subsequently included in Theobald's edition of the plays in 1733.

6. *Works of Shakespear*, ed. Pope (1725), 3:422.

7. "Still Babbling of Green Fields: Mr Greenfields and the Twenty-third Psalm," in *Shakespeare, Text and Theater*, ed. Jay L. Halio, Lois Potter, and Arthur Kinney (Cranbury, NJ: Associated University Presses, 1999), 45–61.

8. "Informations to William Drummond of Hawthorndon," line 157, in *The Cambridge Edition of the Works of Ben Jonson*, ed. David Bevington, Martin Butler, and Ian Donaldson (Cambridge: Cambridge University Press, 2012), 5:370.

9. *The Works of Mr William Shakespear*, ed. Thomas Hanmer (London, 1744), 2:502.

10. S. L. Bethell, *The Winter's Tale: A Study* (London: Staples Press, 1947). For a full discussion see my Oxford *Winter's Tale* (1996), 38–39.

11. *Abraham Ortelius His Epitome of the Theatre of the Worlde* (London, 1603), fol. 52ᵛ.

12. The second story in Barnabe Riche, *Riche His Farwell to the Militarie Profession* (London, 1589).

13. Ortelius, fol. 89ᵛ.

14. Lada Cale Feldman offers evidence that Renaissance Ragusa/Dubrovnik was known for its festival atmosphere and argues that it is therefore an appropriate setting for a play with the title *Twelfth Night*. But this is surely special pleading: Orsino's court is never said to be in Ragusa; it is simply somewhere in Illyria. "Engendered Heritage: Shakespeare's Illyria Travestied," *Narodna umjetnost* 35/1: 215–231 (findable at *hrcak.srce.hr/file/65499*).

15. Note to 3.5.26–28.

8. FOOD FOR THOUGHT

1. George Granville, *The Jew of Venice* (London, 1701), 12.

2. Ibid., 20.

3. *Epigrams* 101, lines 1–16, in *The Cambridge Edition of the Works of Ben Jonson*, ed. David Bevington, Martin Butler, and Ian Donaldson (Cambridge: Cambridge University Press, 2012), 5:166–167.

4. Martial, *Epigrams*, 11.52, lines 13–14, tr. W. A. Ker, Loeb Classical Library (Cambridge, MA: Harvard University Press, 1920).

5. Martial, *Epigrams*, 11.52, lines 16–18.

6. *Epistolae Ho-Elianae. The Familiar Letters of James Howell*, ed. Joseph Jacobs, books II–IV (London: David Nutt, 1892), 403.

7. *Hesperides or Noble Numbers* (1648), 309.

8. The text is that of the Cambridge *Ben Jonson*, 3:555–710.

9. REVISING *KING LEAR*

1. Quotations are from the parallel texts of the Complete Pelican Shakespeare; line references are to this edition.

2. Steven Urkowitz's *Shakespeare's Revision of* King Lear (Princeton: Princeton University Press, 1980) focuses on a number of similar examples. See also Gary Taylor and Michael Warren, eds., *The Division of the Kingdoms* (Oxford: Oxford University Press, 1983); Sidney Thomas, "Shakespeare's Supposed Revision of *King Lear*," *Shakespeare Quarterly* 35.4 (1984): 506–511; Richard Knowles, "Revision Awry in Folio *Lear* 3.1," *Shakespeare Quarterly* 46.1 (1995): 32–46.

3. Sig. G2ʳ. For this and the following other examples, I am indebted to Richard Preiss: "He playes and sings any odde toy" (Robert Greene, *Orlando Furioso* [1594], sig. F4ᵛ); "Jockie is led to whipping over the stage, speaking some word, but of no importance" (Thomas Heywood, *2 Edward IV* [1600], sig. L5ʳ); "Enter Forester, seeing the other taken away; speak anything, and exit" (Anon., *Tryall of Chevalrie* [1605], sig. E4ʳ); "Here they two talk and rail what they list" (John Cooke, *Greenes Tu Quoque* [1614], sig. J1ʳ).

4. *The Plays of William Shakespeare*, eds. Johnson and Steevens (1793), 14:302. Subsequent citations are from this edition.

5. The records of the case were discovered and are discussed by G. W. Boddy, "Players of interludes in North Yorkshire in the early seventeenth century," *North Yorkshire County Record Office Journal*, 3 (1976): 95–130.

6. *The Plays of William Shakespeare*, ed. Samuel Johnson (London, 1765), 207.

7. Anon., "On ye Death of ye Famous Actor R. Burbadge," in C. M. Ingleby et al., *The Shakespeare Allusion Book*, revised ed. (Oxford, 1932), 2 vols., 1:72.

8. Nahum Tate, *The History of King Lear* (1689), 21. Subsequent page references are given in the text.

10. VENICE AT THE GLOBE

1. The classic historical studies are William J. Bouwsma, *Venice and the Defense of Republican Liberty* (Berkeley: University of California Press, 1968) and J. G. A. Pocock, *The Machiavellian Moment* (Princeton: Princeton University Press, 1975). For a more specific study of Thomas and Lewkenor in relation to Shakespeare and Jonson, see David McPherson, *Shakespeare, Jonson, and the Myth of Venice* (Newark, NJ: University of Delaware Press, 1990).

2. 1.1.30–38. The text of *Volpone* is that of *The Cambridge Edition of the Works of Ben Jonson*, ed. David Bevington, Martin Butler, and Ian Donaldson, vol. 3 (Cambridge: Cambridge University Press, 2012). The play is edited by Richard Dutton.

3. Published as *Volpone, Ein Lieblose Komödie* (Potsdam: G. Kiepenheuer, 1926).

4. *Othello*, 1.3.375.

5. "'Tongue-tied, Our Queen?': The Deconstruction of Presence in *The Winter's Tale*", chapter 3 of *The Uses of the Canon: Elizabethan Literature and Contemporary Theory* (Oxford: Oxford University Press, 1992).

6. For the detailed argument, see Stephen Orgel, *Imagining Shakespeare* (Houndmills: Palgrave Macmillan, 2003), chapter 6.

7. Thomas Wilson, *A Discourse upon Usury* (London: Bell, 1925).

8. See page 111.

9. The case is made in detail by Richard Dutton, *Ben Jonson, Volpone and the Gunpowder Plot* (Cambridge: Cambridge University Press, 2008).

11. DANNY SCHEIE'S SHAKESPEARE

1. There is a brief and very informative discussion of the production (including an energetic disagreement with my claim about colonialism) in Jonathan Bate, "Civil Wars in the Rehearsal Room," in *Shakespeare in the Twentieth Century*, ed. Jonathan Bate, Jill L. Levenson, and Dieter Mehl (Newark: University of Delaware Press, 1998), 127–129.

2. There are a couple of exceptions: Titus Andronicus sees through Tamora's impersonation of Revenge, and nobody is deceived by Falstaff's female garments in *The Merry Wives of Windsor*.

3. *New York Times*, February 15, 1995, section C, page 9.

12. SHAKESPEARE ALL'ITALIANA

1. The production had originally been done in the theater's inaugural season, in 2003. As of January 2021, there are four brief scenes from that production on YouTube: Romeo and Benvolio (https://www.youtube.com/watch?v=ea5qDCr4sPo), the ball scene (https://www

.youtube.com/watch?v=B6jEOe1hQxo), the balcony scene (https://www.youtube.com/watch?v=
KIToEOPCyx4), and Romeo's death scene (https://www.youtube.com/watch?v=OBE6X-xflzY).

2. I have been able to locate only two stills of the cast of a revival in 2011, https://static
.rbcasting.com/La-dodicesima-notte-878778.jpg   and   https://abitarearoma.it/globe-theatre-la
-dodicesima-notte-o-quel-che-volete-in-scena-l11-settembre/#pid=1.

Bibliography

This is a bibliography of works that are cited in or bear on the essays in the volume. It includes a number of works that have appeared subsequent to the composition of the essays and which, therefore, though they could not be taken into account, are strictly relevant.

PRIMARY SOURCES

Anon., *The Tryall of Chevalrie*. 1605.

Aubrey, John. *Brief Lives*. Edited by Jack Lynch. http://jacklynch.net/Texts/aubrey-shakespeare.html.

Beaumont, Francis, and John Fletcher. *Comedies and Tragedies*. 1647.

Cooke, John. *Greenes Tu Quoque*. 1614.

Granville, George. *The Jew of Venice*. 1701.

Greene, Robert. *Orlando Furioso*. 1594.

Herrick, Robert. *Hesperides or Noble Numbers*. 1648.

Heywood, Thomas. *The First and Second Partes of King Edward the Fourth*. 1600.

Howell, James. *Epistolae Ho-Elianae. The Familiar Letters of James Howell*. Edited by Joseph Jacobs. 1892.

Jonson, Ben. *The Cambridge Edition of the Works of Ben Jonson*. Edited by David Bevington, Martin Butler, and Ian Donaldson. Cambridge: Cambridge University Press, 2012.

Martial. *Epigrams*. Translated by W. A. Ker, Loeb Classical Library. Cambridge, MA: Harvard University Press, 1920.

Meres, Francis. *Palladis Tamia: Wits Treasury*. 1598.

Ortelius, Abraham. *Abraham Ortelius His Epitome of the Theatre of the Worlde*. 1603.

Pepys, Samuel. *The Diary of Samuel Pepys*. Edited by Robert Latham and William Matthews, vols. 3 and 8. Berkeley: University of California Press, 1970, 1974.

Riche, Barnabe. *Riche His Farwell to the Militarie Profession*. 1589.

Shakespeare, William. *A Collection of Poems . . . Being All the Miscellanies of Mr. William Shakespeare*. Edited by Bernard Lintot. 1709.

———. *The Complete Sonnets and Poems*. Edited by Colin Burrow. Oxford: Oxford University Press, 2002.

———. [*Hamlet*] *Die tragische Geschichte von Hamlet, Prinzen von Dænemark*. Edited by Gerhardt Hauptmann. Weimar: Cranach Presse, 1929.

———. [*King Lear*] *The Complete* King Lear *1608–1623*. Edited by Michael Warren. Berkeley: University of California Press, 1989.

———. *Love's Labour's Lost*. Edited by H. R. Woudhuysen. Arden 3, 1998.

———. *The New Pelican Shakespeare*. Edited by Stephen Orgel and A. R. Braunmuller. New York: Penguin, 2002.

———. *The Plays of William Shakespeare*. Edited by Samuel Johnson. 1765.

———. *The Plays of William Shakespeare*. Edited by Samuel Johnson and George Steevens. 1793.

———. *Poems: Written by Wil. Shakespeare, Gent.* Edited by John Benson. 1640.

———. *Romeo and Juliet. By Shakespear. With alterations, and an Additional Scene: As It Is Performed at the Theatre-Royal in Drury-Lane*. Edited by David Garrick. 1750.

———. [*Romeo and Juliet*] *The First Quarto of Romeo and Juliet*. Edited by Lukas Erne. Cambridge: Cambridge University Press, 2007.

———. *The Sonnets and a Lover's Complaint*. Edited by John Kerrigan. London: Penguin, 1986.

———. [*The Tempest*] *A New Variorum Edition of Shakespeare: The Tempest*. Edited by H. H. Furness. 1892.

———. *The Tempest*. Edited by Frank Kermode. Arden 2, 1954.

———. *The Tempest*. Edited by J. Dover Wilson. Cambridge: Cambridge University Press, 1921.

———. *The Tempest*. Edited by Stephen Orgel. Oxford: Clarendon Press, 1987.

———. *Titus Andronicus*. Edited by Jonathan Bate. Arden 3, 1995.

———. *The Tragedie of Hamlet, Prince of Denmarke*. Edited by J. Dover Wilson. Weimar: Cranach Press, 1930.

———. *The Winter's Tale*. Edited by Stephen Orgel. Oxford: Clarendon Press, 1996.

———. *The Works of Mr William Shakespear*. Edited by Thomas Hanmer. 1744.

———. *The Works of Mr. William Shakespear*. Vols. 1–6 edited by Nicholas Rowe, 1709 and vol. 7 (poems) edited by Charles Gildon. 1710.

———. *Works of Shakespear*. Edited by Alexander Pope. 1725, 1728.

Sidney, Philip. *The Poems*. Edited by William A. Ringler. Oxford: Clarendon Press, 1962.

Spenser, Edmund. *Spenser's Minor Poems*. Edited by Ernest de Sélincourt. Oxford: Clarendon Press, 1910.

Tate, Nahum. *The History of King Lear*. 1689.

Wyatt, Thomas. *Complete Poems*. Edited by Ronald Rebholz. London: Penguin, 1978.

SECONDARY SOURCES

Barbour, Richmond, and Bernhard Klein. "Drama at Sea: A New Look at Shakespeare on the Dragon, 1607–8." In *Travel and Drama in Early Modern England*. Edited by Claire Jowitt and David McInnis, 150–168. Cambridge: Cambridge University Press, 2018.

Bate, Jonathan. "Civil Wars in the Rehearsal Room." In *Shakespeare in the Twentieth Century*. Edited by Jonathan Bate, Jill L. Levenson, and Dieter Mehl, 127–129. Newark: University of Delaware Press, 1998.

Bate, Jonathan, and Russell Jackson, eds. *Shakespeare: An Illustrated Stage History*. Oxford: Oxford University Press, 1996.

Bethell, S. L. *The Winter's Tale: A Study*. London: Staples Press, 1947.

Boddy, G. W. "Players of Interludes in North Yorkshire in the Early Seventeenth Century." *North Yorkshire County Record Office Journal*, 3 (1976): 95–130.

Boeker, Bettina. *Imagining Shakespeare's Original Audience, 1660–2000*. Houndmills: Palgrave Macmillan, 2015.

Booth, Stephen. *Shakespeare's Sonnets*. New Haven: Yale University Press, 1977.

Bosman, Anston. "Mobility." In *Early Modern Theatricality*. Edited by Henry S. Turner, 493–515. Oxford: Oxford University Press, 2013.

———. "Renaissance Intertheater and the Staging of Nobody." *ELH* vol. 71, no. 3 (Fall 2004): 559–585.

———. "Shakespeare and Globalization." In *The New Cambridge Companion to Shakespeare*. Edited by Margreta de Grazia and Stanley Wells, 285–302. Cambridge: Cambridge University Press, 2010.

Bouwsma, William J. *Venice and the Defense of Republican Liberty*. Berkeley: University of California Press, 1968.

Branam, George C. "The Genesis of David Garrick's Romeo and Juliet." *Shakespeare Quarterly* 35.2 (Summer 1984): 170–179.

Braunmuller, A. R. "To the Globe I Rowed": John Holles sees *A Game at Chess*." *English Literary Renaissance* 20 (1990): 340–356.

Coleridge, Samuel Taylor. *Literary Remains*. Edited by H. N. Coleridge. London, 1836.

———. *Seven Lectures on Shakespeare and Milton*. Edited by J. P. Collier. London, 1856.

Cormack, Bradin. "Shakespeare's Narcissus, Sonnet's Echo." In *The Forms of Renaissance Thought*. Edited by Leonard Barkan, Bradin Cormack, and Sean Keilen, 127–149. Houndmills: Palgrave Macmillan, 2009.

De Grazia, Margreta. *Shakespeare Verbatim*. Oxford: Oxford University Press, 1991.

De Grazia, Margreta, and Peter Stallybrass. "The Materiality of the Shakespearean Text." *Shakespeare Quarterly* 44.3 (Autumn 1993): 255–283.

Dobson, Michael. "Shakespeare and Cervantes: Together at Last." In *Cervantes–Shakespeare 1616–2016: Contexto, Influencia, Relación / Context, Influence, Relation*. Edited by J. M. Gonzalez, J. M. Ferri, and M. del Carmen Irles. Berlin: Edition Reichenberger. Teatro del Siglo de Oro. Estudios de Literatura; vol. 129, 9–14.

Dutton, Richard. *Ben Jonson, Volpone and the Gunpowder Plot*. Cambridge: Cambridge University Press, 2008.

Farmer, Alan B. "Playbooks and the Question of Ephemerality." In *The Book in History, the Book as History: New Intersections of the Material Text*. Edited by Heidi Brayman, Jesse M. Lander, and Zachary Lesser, 87–125. New Haven: Beinecke Library, Yale University/Yale University Press, 2016.

Felperin, Howard. *The Uses of the Canon: Elizabethan Literature and Contemporary Theory*. Oxford: Oxford University Press, 1992.

Gillies, John. *Shakespeare and the Geography of Difference*. Cambridge: Cambridge University Press, 1996.

Goldberg, Jonathan. *Shakespeare's Hand*. Minneapolis: University of Minnesota Press, 2002.

———. "'What? In a Names That Which We Call a Rose,' the Desired Texts of *Romeo and Juliet*." In *Crisis in Editing: Texts of the English Renaissance*. Edited by Randall McLeod, 173–202. New York: AMS Press, 1994.

———. *Writing Matter*. Stanford: Stanford University Press, 1990.

Goldstein, David B. *Eating and Ethics in Shakespeare's England*. Cambridge: Cambridge University Press, 2013.

Greenblatt, Stephen. *Shakespearean Negotiations*. Oxford: Clarendon Press, 1998.

Halsey, Katie, and Angus Vine, eds. *Shakespeare and Authority*. Houndmills: Palgrave Macmillan, 2018.

Hazlitt, W. Carew. *Remains of the Early Popular Poetry of England*. London: 1866.

Holland, Peter, and Stephen Orgel, eds. *From Performance to Print in Shakespeare's England*. Houndmills: Palgrave Macmillan, 2006.

———. *From Script to Stage in Early Modern England*. Houndmills: Palgrave Macmillan, 2004.

Hooks, Adam G. "Making Histories; or Shakespeare's *Ring*." In *The Book in History, The Book as History: New Intersections of the Material Text*. Edited by Heidi Brayman, Jesse M. Lander, and Zachary Lesser, 341–373. New Haven: Beinecke Library, Yale University/Yale University Press, 2016.

Ingleby, C. M. et al. *The Shakespeare Allusion Book*, revised ed. Oxford, 1932.

Jackson, Russell, and Robert Smallwood. *Players of Shakespeare 2*. Cambridge: Cambridge University Press, 1988.

Kastan, David Scott. *Shakespeare After Theory*. New York: Routledge, 1999.

———. *Shakespeare and the Book*. Cambridge: Cambridge University Press, 2001.

Kliman, Bernice W. "At Sea About Hamlet at Sea: A Detective Story." *Shakespeare Quarterly* 62 (2011): 180–204.

Knowles, Richard. "Revision Awry in Folio *Lear* 3.1." *Shakespeare Quarterly* 46.1 (1995): 32–46.

Leonard, Alice. *Error in Shakespeare: Shakespeare in Error*. Houndmills: Palgrave Macmillan 2020.

Lesser, Zachary. *"Hamlet" After Q1*. Philadelphia: University of Pennsylvania Press, 2014.

Limon, Jerzy. *Gentlemen of a Company: English Players in Central and Eastern Europe, 1590–1660*. Cambridge: Cambridge University Press, 1985.

Lopez, Jeremy. *Constructing the Canon of Early Modern Drama*. Cambridge: Cambridge University Press, 2014.

Marcus, Leah S. *Unediting the Renaissance*. New York and London: Routledge, 1996.

Marino, James J. *Owning William Shakespeare*. Philadelphia: University of Pennsylvania Press, 2011.

McLeod, Randall. "Un 'Editing' Shak-speare." *SubStance*, vol. 10/11, no. 1, issue 33–34 (1981–1982): 26–55.

McPherson, David. *Shakespeare, Jonson, and the Myth of Venice*. Newark: University of Delaware Press, 1990.

Murphy, Andrew. *Shakespeare in Print*. Cambridge: Cambridge University Press, 2003.

Orgel, Stephen. *The Authentic Shakespeare*. New York: Routledge, 2002.

———. "The Comedian as the Character C." In *English Comedy*. Edited by Michael Cordner, Peter Holland and John Kerrigan, 36–54. Cambridge: Cambridge University Press, 1994.

———. *Imagining Shakespeare*. Houndmills: Palgrave Macmillan, 2003.

———. *Spectacular Performances*. Manchester: Manchester University Press, 2011.

Parkes, Malcolm. *Pause and Effect*. Berkeley: University of California Press, 1993.

Palfrey, Simon, and Tiffany Stern. *Shakespeare in Parts*. Oxford: Oxford University Press, 2007.

Pocock, J. G. A. *The Machiavellian Moment*. Princeton: Princeton University Press, 1975.

Preiss, Richard. *Clowning and Authorship in Early Modern Theatre*. Cambridge: Cambridge University Press, 2014.

Sherman, William H. "Early Modern Punctuation and Modern Editions." *The Book in History, The Book as History: New Intersections of the Material Text*, 303–324. Edited by Heidi Brayman, Jesse M. Lander, and Zachary Lesser. New Haven: Beinecke Library, Yale University/Yale University Press, 2016.

Steevens, George. *The Advertisement to the Plays of William Shakespeare*. 1793.

Stern, Tiffany. *Making Shakespeare*. London and New York: Routledge, 2004.

Taylor, Gary. *Reinventing Shakespeare*. New York: Weidenfeld and Nicolson, 1989.

Taylor, Gary, and Michael Warren. Edited by *The Division of the Kingdoms*. Oxford: Oxford University Press, 1983.

Theobald, Lewis. *Shakespeare Restored*. 1726.

Thomas, Sidney. "Shakespeare's Supposed Revision of *King Lear*." *Shakespeare Quarterly* 35.4 (1984): 506–511.

Urkowitz, Steven. *Shakespeare's Revision of* King Lear. Princeton: Princeton University Press, 1980.

Vickers, Brian. *Shakespeare, A Lover's Complaint, and John Davies of Hereford*. Cambridge: Cambridge University Press, 2007.

Warburg, Aby. "I Costumi Teatrali per gli Intermezzi del 1589." In *Atti dell'Accademia del Reale Istituto Musicale di Firenze: Commemorazione della Riforma Melodrammatica*. Florence, 1895.

Weimann, Robert. *Author's Pen and Actor's Voice*. Cambridge: Cambridge University Press, 2000.

Werstine, Paul. "A Century of 'Bad' Shakespeare Quartos." *Shakespeare Quarterly* 50.3 (Autumn 1999): 310–333.

Williams, Deanne. *Shakespeare and the Performance of Girlhood*. Houndmills: Palgrave Macmillan, 2014.

Williams, G. Walton. "Still Babbling of Green Fields: Mr Greenfields and the Twenty-third Psalm." In *Shakespeare, Text and Theater*. Edited by Jay L. Halio, Lois Potter and Arthur Kinney, 45–61. Cranbury, NJ: Associated University Presses, 1999.

Wilson, Thomas. *A Discourse upon Usury*. Introduction by R. H. Tawney. London: Bell, 1925.

Zweig, Stefan. *Volpone, Ein Lieblose Komödie*. Potsdam: G. Kiepenheuer, 1926.

Index

Acknowledgments

Silvia Bigliazzi of the University of Verona, David Goldstein of York University, Loretta Innocenti of the University of Venice, and Paola Pugliatti of the University of Padua invited me to give the lectures that have eventuated in "Two Household Friends," "Food for Thought," "Lascivious Grace," and "Venice at the Globe." Some of the material in "The Invention of Shakespeare" was first presented at a conference honoring my old friend David Lee Miller at the University of South Carolina. "No Sense of an Ending" was originally conceived as a paper for a Shakespeare Association seminar organized by Bradin Cormack, and "Getting Things Wrong" was written for another Shakespeare Association seminar organized by Anston Bosman. "The Desire and Pursuit of the Whole" was written at the invitation of William Sherman and Barbara Mowat for a special issue of *Shakespeare Quarterly.* The talk that became "Revising *King Lear*" was delivered at a conference on Shakespeare and Samuel Johnson convened by Eric Rasmussen at the University of Nevada, Reno. I am indebted to two anonymous readers, all of whose excellent suggestions for revision I have followed. The dedication records many years of admiration and friendship for one of the great modern Shakespearean scholars.

A few of these essays have previously appeared in print, for the most part in different versions. "The Poetics of Incomprehensibility" is in *Shakespeare Quarterly* 42.4 (Winter 1991), and "The Desire and Pursuit of the Whole" is in *Shakespeare Quarterly* 58.3 (Fall 2007). An earlier version of "Revising *King Lear*" appears under the title "Johnson's *Lear*" in Eric Rasmussen and Aaron Santesso, eds., *Comparative Excellence* (New York: AMS Press, 2007). "Danny Scheie's Shakespeare" combines reviews from *Theatre Journal* 48.1 (March 1996) and *Shakespeare Quarterly* 52.2 (July 2001). A version of "Shakespeare all'italiana" appears in Alison Yarrington, Stefano Villani, and Julia Kelly, eds., *Travels and Translations: Anglo-Italian Cultural Transactions*, Internationale Forschungen zur Allgemeinen und Vergleichenden Literaturwissenschaft (IFAVL), vol. 167 (Rodopi/Brill, 2013). An Italian translation of "Lascivious Grace," "Grazia Lasciva: Il Male che Seduce in Shakespeare e Jonson," is in *Il Piacere del Male*, ed. Paolo Amalfitano (Pisa: Pacini Editore, 2017), and "Venice at the Globe" was published in *SigMa: Revista di Letterature Comparate, Teatro e Arti dello Spettacolo*, vol. 2, 2018.

All quotations from modernized Shakespeare texts are from *The Complete Pelican Shakespeare*, eds. Stephen Orgel and A. R. Braunmuller (New York: Penguin, 2002).

CPSIA information can be obtained
at www.ICGtesting.com
Printed in the USA
JSHW041554010322
23467JS00003B/7